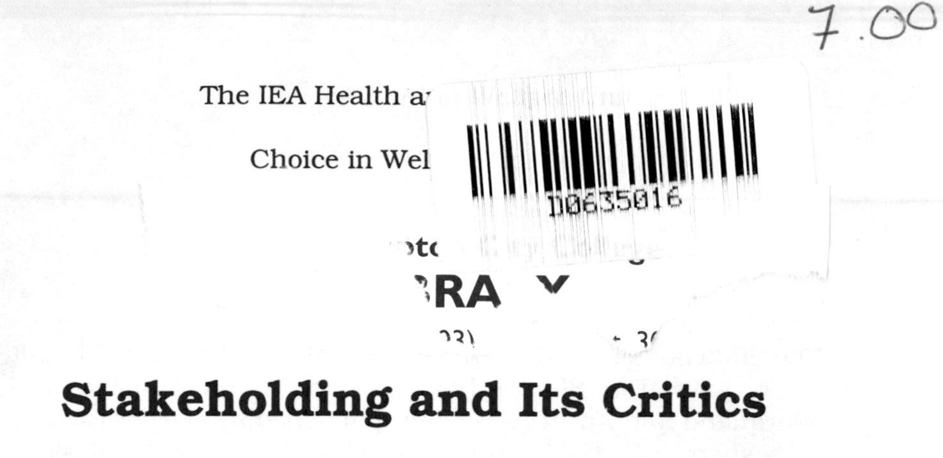

Stakeholding and Its Critics

Will Hutton

Commentaries

Tim Congdon
David G. Green
Sir Stanley Kalms
Martin Ricketts
Elaine Sternberg

First published May 1997

The IEA Health and Welfare Unit
2 Lord North St
London SW1P 3LB

ISBN 0-255 36396-6
ISSN 1362-9565

Typeset by the IEA Health and Welfare Unit
in Bookman 10 point
Printed in Great Britain by
St Edmundsbury Press
Blenheim Industrial Park, Newmarket Road
Bury St Edmunds, Suffolk IP33 3TU

Contents

The Authors

Will Hutton was appointed Editor of *The Observer* in April 1996. He had been assistant editor of the *Guardian* since 1995, having joined the *Guardian* in 1990 as Economics Editor, following ten years at the BBC as producer and correspondent for programmes such as *Newsnight*, *The Money Programme* and *Financial World Tonight*. He was awarded 'Political Journalist of the Year' by Granada TV's *What the Papers Say* in 1993. His book *The State We're In* was published in 1995 and has sat high on the best-seller list ever since. The sequel, *The State to Come*, was published in April 1997. His current appointments are: Chair Employment Policy Institute; Council of the Policy Studies Institute; Council of Institute of Political Economy, University of Sheffield; Editorial Board *New Economy*; Board of London School of Economics; Director of London International Festival of Theatre; Senior Associate Member St. Anthony's College, Oxford, Summer 1993; Visiting Fellow Nuffield College; Visiting Professor Manchester Business School.

Tim Congdon was on the economics staff of *The Times* before joining stockbrokers L. Messel and Co., first as senior economist and then as economics partner. After three years as chief UK economist at Shearson Lehman Hutton, Mr Congdon was appointed economics advisor to Gerrard and National. Since 1989 he has been managing director of Lombard Street Research Ltd., the research subsidiary of Gerrard and National. In 1990 he was appointed Honorary Professor of Economics at Cardiff Business School, and since 1992 he has been a member of the Treasury Panel of Independent Forecasters (the Chancellor's 'wise men'). His books include *Monetary Control in Britain*, 1982, *The Debt Threat*, 1988 and *Reflections on Monetarism* (1992). Mr Congdon is a frequent contributor to the press, particularly *The Times*, on financial matters.

David Green is the Director of the Health and Welfare Unit at the Institute of Economic Affairs. His books include *The Welfare State: For Rich or for Poor?*, 1982; *The New Right: The Counter Revolution in Political, Economic and Social Thought*, 1987; *Equalizing People*, 1990; *Reinventing Civil Society*, 1993; and *Community Without Politics*, 1996. His work has also been published in journals such as the *Journal of Social Policy*, *Political Quarterly*, *Philosophy of the Social Sciences* and *Policy and Politics*.

Sir Stanley Kalms is Chairman of Dixons Group plc, having joined the company in 1948 when it was a one-store family business. Sir Stanley is the founder and sponsor of Dixons Bradford Technology College, and a sponsor of the Chair in Business Ethics and Social Responsibility at the London Business School, where he is an Honorary Fellow, as well as being a Visiting Professor at the North London Business School. He is the Founder of the Stanley Kalms Foundation and co-founder and sponsor of Immanuel College, an independent Jewish secondary school. He is also the founder and sponsor of the Centre for Applied Jewish Ethics in Business and the Professions in Jerusalem. Sir Stanley was awarded a Knighthood in 1996 for services to electrical retailing.

Martin Ricketts is Dean of the School of Business and Professor of Economic Organisation at the University of Buckingham. He has published in the fields of public economics, public policy (especially housing policy) and the new institutional economics. He has been based at the University of Buckingham since 1977. In the years 1991-1992 he was Economic Director of the National Economic Development Office. He is a Trustee and Chairman of the Academic Advisory Council of the Institute of Economic Affairs. He is author of *The Economics of Business Enterprise*, 1986.

Elaine Sternberg earned her PhD in philosophy at the London School of Economics, where she was a Lecturer and a Fulbright Fellow. She spent fourteen years as an investment banker in London, New York and Paris, specialising in international corporate finance and syndicate. The author of *Just Business: Business Ethics in Action*, Little, Brown (UK), 1994; Warner paperback 1995, Dr Sternberg is a Research Fellow in Philosophy at the Centre for Business and Professional Ethics at the University of Leeds, and Principal of Analytical Solutions, a consultancy firm specialising in business ethics and corporate governance. Her book *Corporate Governance: Accountability in the Marketplace*, will be available soon from the IEA.

Foreword

We are very grateful to Will Hutton for accepting our invitation to subject himself to criticism by five commentators. The end result reveals a wide gulf of understanding between the protagonists. Will Hutton insists that he is not a socialist of the old school, nor even anti-market, but rather that he wishes to improve capitalism. He is a sincere man and I take him at his word.

However, there is no better example of the gap in understanding than Will's claim that his critics advocate 'free-market totalitarianism' (p. 89). His reasoning is that free marketeers are supposed to celebrate choice, whereas they oppose choosing to have 'no choice'. The problem seems to be a failure to see that more is at stake in choosing *between* political systems—on the one hand a system that protects individual responsibility (choice) and on the other, one that prefers decisions (choices) to be made by the government—than in making any one of the detailed day-to-day choices that we might make *within* any one system. Will Hutton's assertion is the equivalent of accusing someone who favours religious tolerance of being totalitarian if he is against religious *in*tolerance, because, to be consistently tolerant, he should tolerate intolerance.

The strength of this collection is not, therefore, that it reveals much of a meeting of minds, but rather that it brings together succinct and forthright statements of the contrary views that touch the heart of modern political debate. The contributions by Martin Ricketts and Tim Congdon are outstanding.

We hope that it will be the beginning of a fruitful exchange of views with Will Hutton, and other advocates of stakeholding, about the proper scope and limits of government in a free society.

David G. Green

The Stakeholder Society

Will Hutton

Britain is not succeeding as it should. The difficulty is not its attachment to capitalism; market principles could hardly have been applied more fiercely over the last seventeen years. The problem is more complex, rooted in the highly unproductive way in which British social, economic and governmental structures lock together. The solution is neither to pursue the current path, nor to attempt any return to the failed corporatism of the 1970s. Rather it is to strike out in a new direction altogether, escaping the polarities of collectivism and individualism through which capitalism has so often been analysed and interpreted, towards a new conception of the stakeholder economy and society.

This chapter is a broad outline of the intellectual position I have been developing in newspaper commentaries over the last few years and articulate in my book, *The State We're In.* New Keynesian economic theories offer a new prism through which to interpret the market economy. This, together with the insight that capitalism comes in many forms, differentiated significantly by the ways investment capital is supplied and corporations are governed, provided the theoretical underpinnings both for a critique of the current system—and to guide a new way forward. In the balkanisation and demoralisation of British society, the consequences of the *status quo* are there for all to see—and without change the sustainability of British capitalism will ultimately come under threat. But, on balance, there are grounds for optimism. If the centre and liberal-left can reawaken the tradition of British liberalism that was sundered by twentieth-century socialism, there is every chance that these 'stakeholder' prescriptions will be fulfilled in the years ahead.

The Stakeholding Perspective

Capitalism comes in diverse forms. The simple proposition that the alternative to capitalism is socialism is an inadequate and misleading way of looking at the choices available. There are a multiplicity of capitalisms, configured by their institutional structures and the way the economic, social and political interconnect. Hence there are truly democratic choices available within a capitalist society. The way the left-right argument has been conducted during most of the twentieth century, between planning and the market, socialism and capitalism, is not particularly helpful now, if it ever was. Those are not the choices on offer, and one form of capitalism or another is now the only game in town.

The way forward for the centre and the left is to reawaken a long and honourable progressive tradition, which splintered in the early years of the twentieth century. Just as in the past, the left has done itself a disservice by becoming stuck on the wrong road of public ownership, Conservatives do capitalism no favours with their obsession with a single, pure, free-market theory. It is obvious from the real world that different forms of capitalist system exist. There are varying combinations of the principles of commitment and flexibility, co-operative trust and competitive rigour, in economic life and, just as importantly, in the way states, private institutions and society at large are organised. The congruence of these elements defines the political economy of a capitalist society.

Three models of capitalist society

There are three basic models of capitalism extant in the world today, plus the British variant, which is a less productive form than those that prevail in the United States, East Asia and Europe. The neglected realm of political economy is the key to understanding the plurality of types of capitalism—an intellectual tradition to which *The State We're In* firmly belongs. When individual capitalist systems are seen as a whole, it is the way that the political, economic and social interlock that is striking. Moreover the varying shapes of those intersections determine their character as nations.

The United States is commonly seen as the most individualistic and libertarian of all economies. American financial, labour and product markets are very competitive and free, and public involvement in social welfare and direct ownership is comparatively small. But besides aggressive competition, the institutional structure of the American economy, for instance the existence of over 10,000 regional banks and government support for high-technology research in the defence and space programmes, fosters some level of co-operative endeavour. Decentralised and participatory government is a yardstick for private action as well.

Social-market Europe, perhaps typified by Germany, represents another coherent way of structuring economic, political and social affairs. Unlike the United States, co-operation is entrenched through the mutual recognition of the rights of capital and labour, long-term relationships between borrowers and lenders and a political system based explicitly on formal power sharing. Regional government, and in parallel regional financial institutions, exist and are locked in to the national settlement. There is a generous social state. While this form has inflexibilities, it does conform to market imperatives.

East Asian capitalism takes the combination of co-operative behaviour in a competitive environment to its most extreme, in a way that confuses those accustomed to Anglo-American binary oppositions in logic and economics. Its financial system is regulated, traditional and long-term. Labour is immobile, though trade unions are docile. Firms and the state promote inclusiveness and consensus among their members. Product markets are fiercely competitive but producers build up long-term relations of trust with their suppliers, financiers and work-forces.

In each of these models it is clear that actors such as firms, banks and workers behave in ways that are impossible to explain through classical assumptions about motivation. Behaviour *is* rational, but has to be placed within the context of the entire system of relations which makes up the political economy of the model.

British is not best

The British model is based on the same ideological theories as obtained in the US, but its institutional and political arrangements are vastly different, in ways that produce a less successful outcome for the overall system. In trying to copy America, we have ended up with the worst of both worlds. Britain has neither the dynamism of the USA, nor the institutions of social cohesion and long-term investment found in Europe.

The problems with the British approach date back to the way the country industrialised during the eighteenth century, in a largely spontaneous and market driven way, without state action (although there was more state support than most historians recognise). This contrasts sharply with industrial development in Germany and Japan. The institutions of British economy and society have never been configured to encourage industrial investment and progress. The relationship between British finance and industry has long been destructive, with finance usually triumphant. The City of London has always been dominant, both for domestic reasons and because of London's role as an international financial centre.

The property that defines the British financial system is its overarching preoccupation with liquidity (the capacity to turn loans and investments into cash rapidly). This flexibility is in the interests of finance and the markets that have been constructed to enable assets to be quickly cashed; but it is not in the interests of producers, who require more commitment. Short-term risks and high rates of return are the key features of British finance. This not only makes investment problematic, but puts companies under constant threat of takeover if they try to adopt other priorities than achieving high short-term returns.

Social values in Britain have long privileged finance over industry, and thus formed part of a failing overall system. The respect given to effortless superiority, the word of honour, the subtleties of rank and class, and aristocratic invisible income has a strong hold in British culture and accords with success at finance, commerce and administration rather than laboriously making products. Britain has been in thrall to 'gentlemanly capitalism' for most of this century, and only an interlude between 1931 to 1951, when depression and war forced the real economy's interests to be asserted, has offered partial relief.

British companies are subject to an arbitrary executive, to financial priorities above all others, and are subordinated to the pursuit of short-term profit. The function of the British company, in contrast to the Japanese firm, is to generate a high rate of return from trading activity, rather than to be a productive organisation embedded in a network of long-term trust relations—including financiers and work-force alike. The stock market's facilitation of hostile takeovers, and its inability to price future income rationally, police the firm's attachment to short-term returns. That the vast majority of important British firms are public companies largely owned by institutional shareholders whose aim is to extract dividends and capital gains is one of the most salient facts about the British economy. In Japan, share-holding is an expression of commitment and interlocking interests, and in other Asian economies the family firm is the primary unit.

The pre-modern, quasi-feudal British state is part of the systemic problem. Its economic institutions, the Treasury and the Bank of England, are part of the nexus of financial interests favouring gentlemanly rentierdom. Social, financial and governmental power are all centralised in London and the state has shown itself incapable of being other than *dirigiste* and centralised. It is the fount of the problems Britain has in defining responsible institutions. The state conforms to no agreed rules and has no clear set of principles governing its relationship with, and responsibilities to, its citizens. It need pay no heed to any concerns save the self-interest of the ruling party, malleable 'public opinion' and the book-keeping values of the Treasury. Attempts to create co-operative institutions, social rights and responsibilities, and regulation in the public interest have failed in Britain because of the fundamental lack of these values at the core of the state. This, again, is in sharp contrast to successful capitalist models, where the role of the state is delineated in a written constitution.

In Britain, unlike America, Europe or East Asia, the political, social and economic systems form a whole which is not conducive to industrial success and social cohesion. This is not to argue that everything in Britain is failing and everything is working perfectly abroad; but it *is* to assert that enough is going wrong in Britain to arouse powerful concern—and overseas models offer insights and structures which, although they cannot be imported wholesale, need to be carefully examined for their lessons.

Conservative Britain has followed the wrong track ...

Many of the faults with the British system have been accentuated by the policies of successive Conservative governments since 1979. Conservative supremacy was used for the single-minded pursuit of free-market economic doctrines: the retreat of the state and the ungloving of the invisible hand of market forces were supposed to create a new era of prosperity free from the 'distortions' caused by government intervention.

The results have proved different, and have not been due to a lack of thoroughness in the implementation of free-market reforms. The state has been purged of people and institutions which supported other priorities and the possibilities inherent in a system of government unregulated by written norms have been exploited to the full.

The financial system was almost completely deregulated in a series of changes, such as the lifting of exchange controls and the scrapping of banks' reserve requirements. Instead of a new age of investment, this led to a surge in consumer and housing lending, while industry's capital stock per unit of output declined. The dominance of finance over the real economy was strengthened, as high real interest rates—the only lid on credit once controls had gone—inhibited investment and rewarded the rentier.

Labour market reforms were intended to bring it closer to the classical ideal of a market, by allowing workers to 'price themselves into jobs' and causing the market to clear. Therefore, trade unions' powers were systematically restricted, and benefits cut to try to eliminate 'scrounging'. After nearly two decades of this process, the promised results have still not appeared—the numbers unemployed or economically inactive remain high and wages are still unresponsive to changes in unemployment. The theory was fundamentally wrong in imagining that the labour market was a market like all others, that wages are compensation for work which is inherently unpleasant, and that the human values of fairness and motivation are irrelevant. Exhaustive academic research has found, for example, that employers pay wages above the lowest possible level and are slow to sack workers in recessions because they place a high value on loyalty, fairness and the construction of effective teams. Free-market theory has proved inadequate at explaining such apparently irrational behaviour.

... and created a new world of them and us

Poverty and insecurity have resulted from Conservative labour market and social security policies. The segmentation of the labour market has created a new and pernicious form of social stratification: the 30-30-40 society. Approximately 30 per cent of the population are disadvantaged; the unemployed, those excluded from the labour market and those with only the most marginal participation. As in the US, the poverty and social stress experienced by this group of people causes acute misery and has consequences for the rest of society. Crime, family breakdown, a growing army of only partially socialised young men and vast social security spending on propping up inequality are the result.

The next 30 per cent are the marginalised and the insecure, whose jobs, for one reason or another, do not provide any tenure. This includes households dependent on part-time earnings (up to two years), those under short-term contracts with few employment rights, and those who have become involuntarily self-employed. This category is particularly exposed to the spread of marketisation and the displacement of risk onto individuals, who have found it extremely difficult to cope with the necessity for private pensions, health insurance and transport.

The remaining 40 per cent are the privileged, with tenured employment, although this group are by no means uniformly wealthy. They are often the insiders of more sophisticated labour market theories, who have enough power to do well.

This sort of society is economically unproductive as well as morally repugnant. Keynesian economists have always pointed out that unequal societies are more prone to underconsumption and hence harsher fluctuations of the economic cycle, because higher savings rates among the rich lower general effective demand. The tax system has become systematically less progressive, with particular bonanzas for wealthy individuals and the corporate sector, most notably oil companies. For the poorest in society, spending is skewed towards VAT-exempt and zero-rated goods and the informal economy. The result has been a severe deterioration in the growth of tax revenues and the ability of the government to afford its programmes without increasing taxes on those in the middle of the range.

... because it has followed bizarre economic doctrines

The theoretical concepts that have been adduced in support of this policy direction are almost embarrassingly flimsy. The first building block has been the so-called 'rational economic man', a creature unknown to anyone who has spent half an hour studying human psychology. This imaginary creature values work negatively and leisure positively; he exists to maximise his own utility and has a clear concept of how this can be achieved given the alternatives available.

Supply and demand certainly interact in markets, but the elegant classical pattern of scissors crossing at an equilibrium point is not supported by the observations of real-world research. Indeed the marginal costs of production can fall when greater quantities are supplied, across a wide range of industries—so that both demand and supply curves actually end up sloping in the same direction.

In some ways the worst error is to believe in a general competitive equilibrium; that a free-market system will itself arrive at an unimprovable optimum point under its own steam. The assumptions required to reach this result in pure theory are extremely distant from the conditions pertaining in real markets, and involve bizarre abstractions like omniscience, a universal auctioneer, and the suspension of the passage of time. This is so extreme that competitive equilibrium theory tells us nothing about the dynamics of market economics.

Britain should adopt the concept of stakeholding

Economics instead should be based on the realities of capitalist societies. This involves explaining phenomena such as the business cycle, corporate behaviour, and the way in which economic systems interlock with the social and political. The work of John Maynard Keynes is at the root of this alternative economic tradition.

The prescriptions of such an approach are very different from those of free-market theory. They involve an observation of what differentiates successful from unsuccessful forms of capitalism, a question that revolves around investment. This in turn is crucially linked to the organisation of the financial system, which in Britain should be reformed in order to lower the cost of capital and lengthen the payback period required of investment projects. It would involve wholesale restructuring under the aegis of a reformed Bank of England, to establish patterns of more committed ownership and more long-term lending.

A multiplicity of small reforms, ranging from the role of non-executive directors to the tax treatment of short-term capital gains, would help to push the system towards generating more committed, patient owners and bankers. A network of thriving regional and specialist banks could be encouraged, but that, in turn, is predicated on the way shareholding is regarded and whether it can be transformed into a stable relationship of commitment; and an end to the way in which a single loan can make a firm the prisoner of the bank, without the bank in turn having any responsibility or stake in the firm's success. The tax system should promote long-term shareholding and penalise speculation, and there should be other legal and financial obstacles to takeovers. Company accounts should become more transparent, and corporate governance reformed to reflect the various interests that converge on the firm—suppliers, workers and trade unions, banks, as well as shareholders and directors. This is the central idea of the stakeholder economy.

The choice now is not to return to the debased corporatism of the 1970s, but to develop a capitalism that is socially cohesive and economically productive. Part of the process of ideological self-definition is finding a word to describe the variety of capitalism one is championing, and stakeholding is an attractive choice. The idea has long been deployed in management literature and various firms have described themselves as stakeholder companies. The best types of overseas forms of capitalism have been achieved by striking the right balance between commitment and flexibility. Stakeholding is a neat way of encapsulating just that.

The welfare state should be restructured

The success of a stakeholder economy is dependent on the creation of a stakeholder society. The welfare state is a potentially powerful means of expressing national social solidarity, but is progressively at risk as it becomes organised around means testing and creeping marketisation. Yet a welfare system worthy of the name depends upon a national consensus, and this is unlikely to develop around either a flimsy safety net or an overly restrictive and uniform system. Stopping the fragmentation of society, by imbuing the successful with a sense of common social citizenship, requires recognising their desires for self-advancement.

This means that equality of provision needs to be surrendered before the larger necessity of universal inclusion; that some measure of inequality has to be traded off against universality of membership. The state should offer supplementary social insurance systems in unemployment benefit and health which would take provision beyond the universal minimum, in a similar way to the pension system offered under the old SERPS. Catering for excellence in the public sphere also means recognising that while access to schools should be egalitarian, setting and streaming need to be introduced as key exams are approached to emphasise that academic excellence rather than social engineering is the objective of the state education system. Much better to have the middle-class attending grammar schools and streamed comprehensives than opting out into élite-forming private schools.

Stakeholding means a written constitution too ...

Social and economic developments are obviously embedded in the character of the political system. Britain's lack of a written constitution, and the behaviour of its state, is a prime generator of the values and practices that are prevalent throughout society. For many years the pressure for constitutional reform has been directed at individual issues, whether it is a proportional voting system or a Bill of Rights, and the arguments used have been specific. Now they are coming together. As British ministers try to claim that European justice should have 'variable geometry' and the Scott Report and the BSE fiasco highlight the failures of secretive and unaccountable government, constitutional reform has been brought into the mainstream of peoples' concerns and made into the subject of political debate.

Co-operative, successful forms of capitalism do not arise spontaneously, but are the product of conscious design. To engage in such a reform programme government must have the democratic legitimacy—based on the principles of proportionality, inclusiveness and openness rather than winner-take-all triumphalism. In consequence, unions, companies and other private interest might just accept regulation and intervention as being more than just the impositions of partisan state. Britain needs to acquire a republican attitude—not in terms of abolishing the monarchy, but rather in reclaiming the idea that government is a matter for the public, not a secretive élite.

The poverty of British constitutional arrangements is apparent when one considers their inability to enable effective mediating institutions between the central state and the citizen. An independent Bank of England under current arrangements would be a shadow of central banks elsewhere, most likely falling under the ever more total control of London finance and the Conservative Party power network. A democratised Bank should reflect the political, regional and economic pluralism of a democratised policy. Diffused executive power in Britain, through institutions such as Training and Enterprise Councils, hospital trusts and quangos need not be a pernicious development, as it is when party bias, bookkeeping values and secrecy pervade their operations. A decentralisation of political power would foster a decentralisation of financial power.

The British state has no rules or guiding principles, and it is not surprising that this lacuna is found elsewhere in society—we are subjects and workers, not citizens and members of productive teams. Running a company is a reflection of running the nation—it is dominated by the executive, audit is weak, an extremely feeble form of shareholder democracy is the nominal final arbiter, and a narrow view is taken of wider responsibilities to stakeholders.

This is the prescriptive part of the argument that economic, political and social systems should work hand in hand. It is about reinventing the liberal, Whig tradition in British politics. Liberals at the turn of the century fragmented and variously allied with labour or 'gentlemanly capital', but at the end of the twentieth century there is the opportunity to regroup. John Monks, of the TUC, for example, and Iain Vallance of BT come from a bigger shared tradition than the camps of twentieth-century socialism or free-market purism. The dormant Whig tradition is one that can be productive and progressive.

... and engagement with foreign affairs

There are certainly consequences for foreign policy and international economic relations if Britain is to be changed in this fashion. The stable post-war order was underpinned by international co-operation around American leadership, within the stable exchange rate system of Bretton Woods. International financial flows are now so large as to be beyond the control of any government; in order to allow countries to make their own choices there has to be an international structure of control. Private capital does need freedom of movement, but within a framework of standardised environmental and employment rights, which would prevent a destructive auction of immiseration in the interests of unaccountable finance. The restoration of the European ideal—and the creation of a popular democratic consciousness within Europe—is necessary if sovereignty over economic life is to be reasserted. It also implies a commitment to international order, through resistance to aggression rather than the weak policies seen during the wars in the former Yugoslavia. Economic and political order are indivisible—sustaining a moral diplomatic order is a vital precondition of economic prosperity.

Originality and Influences

The State We're In is a work of synthesis, of my own ideas and those of others. Its objective is to draw the connection between the failures of corporate and political systems of governance and the effect that has had on the labour market and therefore British society generally. But I couldn't make any of those steps of the argument without having the facts, theory and research of hundreds of people at my disposal as support for what I am saying. When a tide of ideas is turning, the intellectual enquiry of people in many different areas links up in sometimes surprising ways. For example, sociologists of the family have become interested in what is happening in the labour market because of the effects of deregulation—the commitment to being a good parent in market societies is becoming more and more difficult. Equally, geographers have taken an increasing interest in my concerns about the centralisation of the British financial system, and its effect on regional economies. I have been very privileged in my years at the *Guardian* to have seen the products of a lot of different intellectual supply lines cross my desk, and to try to knit the strands together.

Keynes offers the outstanding alternative to free-market theory, and much of the underpinning of my economic analysis is due to him, augmented by the insights of modern game theory. His *General Theory* is the book that has had the largest single influence on my thought. In contrast to the unreal abstractions of free-market theory, Keynes attempted to account for the actual realities of capitalism. The focus of his attention was on the place where time, money and uncertainty—all crucial facts about life that classical theorists assumed away—intersect and have the greatest impact. This is the financial system, which is supposed to reconcile the conflicting interests of savers and investors, and therefore has a powerful influence on the most volatile element of the economy, namely investment. This is the origin of my concern with the financial system as a determinant of economic success. The Keynesian tradition is much richer and has more explicatory power than the bastardised versions which have reached textbooks, and the straw man created by its intellectual opponents. As interpreted by Axel Leijonhufvud and James Meade it is simply the economics of reality. In recent years, some American economists have pioneered a remarkable resurgence of these ideas, based on new insights, which have started to transform academic thinking. Part of my work in my columns has been to disseminate this thinking to a wider audience.

Professor John Kay wrote *The Foundations of Corporate Success*, which focused on company architecture as a determinant of company growth, a good year before I wrote *The State We're In*. David Goodhart wrote a good paper for the IPPR (The Institute of Public Policy Research) on German stakeholder capitalism, while David Marquand's important book, *The Unprincipled Society*, was a forerunner of some of the principal arguments. All three were important intellectual influences.

My ideal, in terms of the traditional spectrum between collectivism and individualism, is different, forming the third point of a conceptual triangle:

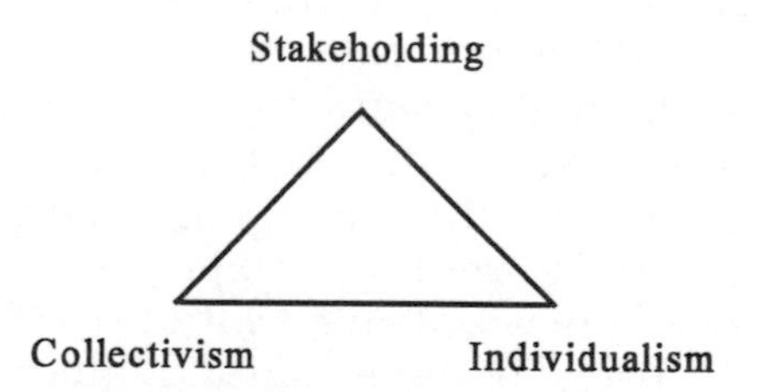

This is different from, say, a classic compromise position such as that found in Harold Macmillan's famous book *The Middle Way*, which struck a balance between the traditions of collectivism and individualism. He would compromise with socialists over nationalisation, arguing that a public good should be in public ownership. In contrast, I would dispute that public ownership is necessary on those grounds. If you can structure a firm well, you do not need public ownership. A stakeholder firm incorporates the social partnership and dialogue that you are trying to achieve. There may be technical reasons for a public monopoly to be publicly owned, but these are entirely technical.

I hope stakeholding can reawaken the liberal tradition and escape collectivism. For example, it should be possible to criticise British company law for being inadequate because it does not define the job of non-executive directors without being accused of promoting socialism. This is a liberal reformist statement, not, as it is interpreted by many businessmen, a death threat to modern British capitalism.

The Prospects for Success

In the past, only traumatic events like defeat in war, economic collapse or revolution have given a country a sufficient shock to adopt the wide ranging and radical change which Britain must choose now. Britain failed, for historical reasons, to renew itself, while America, France, the rest of Europe, and east Asia have performed this feat in the last 250 years. Over two centuries late, it is time for the spirit of 1789 to arrive in Britain and democratise government and society; the euthanasia of the rentier can be achieved without the guillotine.

Confronting an established order, even when it has demonstrably failed, is always a daunting process. Centuries of power and privilege have embedded the elite networks which underpin Conservatism and the rentier state. Consecutive years of power have entrenched Conservative ideological hegemony and spread its supporters throughout the media and business worlds, as well as the ramshackle maze that comprises the British state. Politicised influence is now entwined with the old networks. An entire failed system needs to be reshaped, requiring effort across the range of policy areas. It is entirely predictable that the resistance to a reform programme would be determined and hysterical, and election campaigns fought during such a confrontation will be brutal.

But Britain has the opportunity to achieve change and the prospects should be a cause for optimism. The country led the world in industrialisation and parliamentary democracy, and can lead in peaceful democratic renewal. The conditions now are positive. The failure of the Conservative project to produce the results it promised, on its own terms, let alone when subjected to a wider critique, strip away the economic reasons which may have generated support. The Conservative revolution is consuming its own; the monarchy and other traditional institutions are in decline, and the little platoons, such as voluntary organisations and even English counties, are being disbanded as the market and the centralising state apply their inexorable formulae. The Conservative Party has been in internal crisis, with Britain's role in Europe serving as a focus for deeper incoherence.

Under the leadership of Tony Blair, the Labour Party has attempted to build a wider consensus around the progressive pole in British politics, although perhaps at the cost of a radical reforming vision. The election may mark the start of the programme, although the mandate for a full radical reform might not take shape until after a first term of more cautious progress. Blair is trying to convey the idea that the Labour Party is travelling in an individualist direction while espousing collective values, but only occasionally does he travel into a new ideological space, by talking about political reform and the enabling state as the handmaiden of economic and social change. He is by no means a consistent follower of the entire agenda, and has made it known that his espousal of stakeholding is not the same as buying the programme of *The State We're In.* On the other hand, he uses the same language and concepts, and setting the agenda is the first battle in politics.

Some of the finest academic economists in Britain—John Kay, Steve Nickell and Richard Layard—are trying to elaborate a theoretical programme of research which has shared preoccupations with these lines of thought, linking the structure of finance and corporate government to investment and growth. Extraordinarily, given its importance to the way the world works, this is a research area that economics has neglected over the last twenty years. In the United States, some Democrats have been considering radical change to corporate governance and the tax system to promote responsibility from private firms.

The concepts and preoccupations outlined in *The State We're In*, and the growing body of writing and research on its themes, are reaching a wider and wider audience. My hope is that it can contribute to the change it advocates, and I am very optimistic about success. Stakeholding is finding an increasingly positive reception among industrial and even financial audiences. Whether it is private seminars in the City or strategy meetings of the police force, the ideas are debated—and more sympathetically than ever seemed likely on publication. It may be written from the centre-left tradition, but immense numbers of the British immediately understand its themes—and relate to it. Even the right have to concede that it is passing the market test.

On balance, it is probable that we will get the political change that is necessary. Economic restructuring can happen. Britain could become the dynamic and socially cohesive place which its population yearns to live in—but it will take nerve and grit. The rewards could be immense.

Commentaries

How Britain Benefits from Short-termism

Tim Congdon

Mr Will Hutton's best-selling book, *The State We're In*, has brought together in a single volume many widely-held prejudices about modern Britain. Whatever the merits of these prejudices, his achievement is to have assembled them in the form of a book so that it can serve as a focus for debate. In particular, Hutton repeats and develops a number of popular criticisms of Britain's financial institutions. He may be the first author to present a sustained argument—in a piece longer than a newspaper article—that the British financial system suffers from 'short-termism'. The phrase has been used many times, but now at last someone has spelt out in detail what it means.

According to Hutton, 'The British economy is organised around a stock-market-based financial system and clearing banks averse to risk'.[1] As a result, the financial system is—in his view—'disengaged' from and 'uncommitted' to industry, and is 'uniquely bad at supporting investment and innovation'. While these British weaknesses are said to have a long historical pedigree, Hutton alleges that the financial system has done particular harm since 1979. The Thatcher Government's programme of deregulation and privatisation is said to have enhanced the power of the financial system over the corporate sector. In Hutton's opinion, from 1980 onwards '[t]he economy was to be vandalised by the financial sector in the name of market freedom'.[2] Of course, 'the City'—as the hub of the British financial system—is strongly attacked.

How serious is Hutton's indictment? Is he right to claim that the financial system has let Britain down and, if there has been damage to the economy, has it been greater since 1979 than before?

The State We're In is attractively written. But the flow of phrases, and the extraordinary range and ambition of the book, make it difficult to pinpoint the main themes of Hutton's critique. For example, towards the end of chapter one Hutton remarks, '[t]o break out of this cycle of decline and to build cooperative institutions, Britain must complete the unfinished business of the seventeenth century'.[3] This proposition is paradoxical and astonishing, and a joy to debate. However, it suffers from a serious drawback: it cannot be subjected to a simple empirical test. Indeed, although at the first reading the opening five chapters are great fun and appear to 'say something', on a second or third reading they dissolve. They say nothing that could be recognised as a refutable criticism of the City or the British financial system or, to be honest, of any feature of the British economy.

This may seem too dismissive, but Hutton's problem is that most of the institutions that he regards as specific to Britain, and the source of its woes, are in fact common to all Western societies. These societies are uniform in their adherence to the rule of law, the dominance of market forces in price determination and a financial system based on private property. It is absurd for Hutton to single out Britain for its dependence on 'gentlemen', 'gentlemanly capitalists', 'market forces', 'the maximisation of shareholder value' and such like. Every Western society has them.

Hutton may be right that certain arrangements associated with a market economy came first in Britain; he may have a point when he suggests that these arrangements are deeply entrenched. But his interpretation of history could be turned on its head. It could be that Britain pioneered the industrial revolution and parliamentary democracy precisely because it was the first society to uphold personal freedom and individual responsibility, and to defend so consciously the related concepts of private property and market forces.[4] Further, it may be that other societies have been able to catch up with Britain economically over the last 125 years only because they have copied these hallmarks of its society.

If so, Britain's triumph was to demonstrate the superiority of a free-market economic system over the medieval structures of its European neighbours and pre-Meiji Japan, with their feudal stakeholder attributes. Capitalism could validly be associated with modernity, the open society and all those successful structures (market freedom, individualism and so on) to which Hutton is so hostile in a British context; cooperation and 'the stakeholder economy' could be stigmatized as relics of medievalism and, at a further remove, of the tribal society.

Unfortunately, neither this sort of defence of Britain's past record nor Hutton's attack on it can be assessed by a simple and rigorous statistical test. As opinion, the first five chapters are interesting and amusing; from an analytical standpoint, they are irrelevant and can be discarded. If the historical baggage in the early chapters is dumped as impossible to analyse in a structured way, Hutton's substantive criticism of the British financial system must lie in the rest of the book. But chapters seven to nine say little about the organisation of the financial system, chapter ten is mostly about foreign capitalisms and chapter eleven reviews 'The republican opportunity'. That leaves chapter six on 'Tomorrow's money today' and chapter twelve on 'Stakeholder capitalism' as containing the essence of Hutton's case. If he has something worthwhile to say, it must be in these two chapters. The rest of this paper concentrates on chapter six, because it introduces a new and possibly important topic in economic theory, and presents the core of the attack on short-termism.

The 'Fetish' of Liquidity

The chapter starts with the claim that: 'The overriding property of the [British] system is its desire for liquidity—in other words, the ability to be able [*sic*] to reverse a lending or investment decision and return to the *status quo ante* of holding cash'. While conceding that every financial system must have this characteristic to some degree, he suggests that Britain's distinctiveness is that 'liquidity has become a fetish', which reflects investors' 'lack of commitment'. So when 'the going gets tough', investors sell their shares and banks withdraw loans, rather than 'share the risk of restructuring and of managing any crisis'. It follows, according to Hutton, that the British system has 'a permanent bias' to short-termism and 'from this all else flows'.[5]

Hutton points an accusatory finger at investors in corporate equity as being particularly short-termist. He seems to regard it as a misfortune that one of the most liquid assets in capitalist societies is corporate equity listed on a stock market. Indeed, Hutton criticizes venture capitalists for sometimes putting pressure on successful innovative companies to float on the stock market, which may be 'bad for the individual company's longer-term prospects'.[6] Once they are listed on the stock market, companies are vulnerable to take-over, which again—according to Hutton—may interfere with long-term planning.

The attack on liquidity is the consistent theme of the first half of chapter six. No previous author has suggested so explicitly that financial market liquidity may be bad for economic efficiency. There have been earlier statements of the idea, but they have been much briefer, less considered and more piecemeal. Tobin has recommended that a tax be placed on foreign exchange trading, because 'sand in the wheels' would reduce excessive turnover and harmful speculation, but he has limited his fiscal proposal to the foreign exchanges.[7] Further back, chapter 12 of Keynes *General Theory*, on 'The state of long-term expectation', included a number of derogatory comments about liquidity. One particularly striking assertion is that:

> Of the maxims of orthodox finance none, surely, is more anti-social than the fetish of liquidity, the doctrine that it is a positive virtue on the part of investment institutions to concentrate their resources upon the holding of 'liquid securities'.

Keynes also proposed—many years before Tobin—that '[t]he introduction of a substantial government transfer tax on all [stock market] transactions' might prove 'most serviceable', in order to curb the 'casino' element.[8]

But Hutton is the first author to present a deliberate and sustained critique of financial market liquidity. The critique raises interesting issues for social organisation, notably for the questions of whether and how secondary trading in financial markets benefits society. Most defences of financial markets are expressed in terms of the improvement in resource allocation achieved in the primary markets (i.e., when shares and bonds are issued, and bank loans disbursed). But they say less, or nothing at all, about how society gains from secondary market activity (i.e., the buying and selling of shares and bonds once they exist). Secondary market activity itself takes up resources, with incomes in stock-broking and investment banking being in most capitalist societies well above those in other walks of life. Hutton's critique prompts the question, 'does society gain anything from trading in secondary financial markets or is such trading, with its Huttonite "fetish of liquidity", parasitic on the rest of society?'. Much of the saloon-bar criticism of the City is undoubtedly spurred by resentment of financial sector incomes. Does Hutton's book provide a respectable intellectual rationale for the claim that secondary financial markets are indeed parasitic?

Short-termism and Under-investment

The second half of chapter six extends the critique of the British financial system by arguing that its short-term focus leads to demands for unduly high rates of return. Hutton claims:

> The more intensively shares are traded, the more widely dispersed ownership becomes; the greater the threat of contested takeover, then the higher the premium companies feel they must earn in order to keep the shareholders happy. This is the fundamental weakness of the British system. British companies not only suffer one of the highest costs of capital in the world, but the febrile stock market compels them to earn a very big mark-up over even that cost of capital to fend off the threat of takeover and keep their shareholder base stable.[9]

To summarize Hutton's position, Britain's financial system requires its companies to achieve such high rates of return on capital that only a few capital projects qualify. He believes that, as a result, British companies under-invest compared with their international competitors, and British workers therefore use less advanced machinery and have lower output per head.

This is not to say that Hutton sticks doggedly to his central idea. Having characterised widely-dispersed share ownership as 'the fundamental weakness',[10] he alleges that a rather different point, the 'lack of rationality about the future', is 'at the heart of the problem'.[11] Hutton cites work by Miles which purports to show that the stock market values returns stretching beyond a year 'less highly than it should'. In consequence, 'payback periods are shorter, target rates of return are higher and dividend pay-outs bigger than in other industrial countries so that British shareholders are disproportionately highly rewarded for the "risks" they run'.[12] The City's international outlook is identified as a further handicap on British industry. In Hutton's view, the trouble is that the City can seek good, high-yielding investments in any country. As a result, 'British companies have to compete ... with the highest returns in the world if they are to get financial support'. The disadvantage of Britain's 'highly marketised' financial system, with its global perspective, is that companies 'have to deliver insane rates of return to their owners'.[13]

As the pages flash by, the link between financial markets' over-emphasis on liquidity (in the first half of chapter six) and the excessively high required rates of return (in the second half) begins to get lost. But concern about the under-valuation of future earnings streams and the City's internationalism is not new. If Hutton has anything original to add to the public debate, it is his proposed link between financial asset liquidity and the returns on physical capital. The core Huttonite principle, the crux of his attack on short-termism, is that the greater the liquidity of financial assets, the higher is the required return on physical capital.

The trouble with Hutton's theory is simple: it is plain wrong. Moreover, it is not wrong in a small way because of a missing detail or an under-emphasized but vital qualification. Instead it is thoroughly wrong, the precise opposite of the truth. Hutton claims a positive relationship between the liquidity of financial assets and the rate of return on physical capital. In fact, the relationship between these two variables is inverse. This is easy to demonstrate. A short digression into the subject of portfolio choice may be helpful.

Consider an investor running a portfolio. As is well-known, his choice can be analysed in terms of a trade-off between return and risk, usually measured by the variance of the return around its expected mean.[14] The investor may of course forego high returns in order to reduce risk. The literature on mean-variance analysis asks interesting questions about the social cost of risk, raising the possibility that a nation may suffer low growth because its investors are too risk-averse. Hutton might have had a valid and interesting case if he had claimed that 'the British Establishment' had historically chosen safe, low-return, 'gentlemanly' investments instead of risky, high-return 'industrial' investments. But that is not what he has done. (If he had done this, he should have objected not to the high returns sought by British investors, but to their lowness.)[15]

Mean-variance analysis forms a large part of the modern theory of portfolio choice. But it neglects a vitally important dimension of the subject. In practice an investor also has a trade-off between return and liquidity. Admittedly, liquidity is a more impalpable concept than risk. It could be defined, following Hutton's perfectly satisfactory suggestion, as 'the ability to reverse a lending or investment decision' and return to cash. Alternatively, it could be expressed more formally as the ratio of the dealing spread to the middle price quoted in a recognised marketplace.[16] (It could even be elaborated as a quite complicated function of the dependence of the spread/middle price ratio on the length of the trading period or the size of the transaction.)

High Liquidity, Low Return

But—however liquidity is described—one point is definite. The higher the asset's liquidity, the lower the expected rate of return an investor will accept. Of course, the most liquid asset in any economy is money. As institutional investors' return patterns demonstrate, cash is the worst performing asset in the long run. (See Table 1, p. 33.) More generally, an investor will accept

1. a lower expected return on a liquid security than on an illiquid security, when considering the choice in markets for quoted securities, and
2. a lower expected return on a quoted security (or a portfolio of quoted securities) than on an unquoted security (or a portfolio of unquoted securities, such as a venture capital fund).

It follows that a society with highly liquid financial markets will tend to have lower rates of return on capital than a society with highly illiquid financial markets; and that a society with organised secondary markets where assets can be traded in securitised form will also tend to have lower rates of return on capital than a society where assets cannot be so traded.

Hutton is particularly misguided when he criticises venture capitalists for urging successful entrepreneurs to list their companies on stock markets. As all venture capitalist know, quoted companies are valued at higher multiples of their earnings than unquoted companies that can be bought and sold only 'in the trade market' (i.e., by other entrepreneurs or companies). A large part of the explanation for the valuation premium commanded by quoted companies is that it is easier to buy and sell their shares. As the higher valuation of corporate equity reduces the company's cost of finance, the required return on capital is lowered by the extra liquidity conferred by a stock market quotation. The corporate finance department of the accountancy firm BDO Stoy Hayward maintains an index of price/earnings (P/E) ratios of private companies in the trade market, based on data in the magazine *Acquisitions Monthly*. This chart is reproduce on p. 36. It shows that the P/E ratio on the stock market as a whole is typically 60 to 80 per cent higher than on private unquoted companies.

It is rather funny that Hutton's book, with its assault on liquidity, should have been receiving so much favourable comment just as the scandal broke over Morgan Grenfell's European unit trust, run by the disgraced fund manager Mr Peter Young. Mr Young's folly was to invest his unit-holder's money in unquoted, and hence illiquid, companies. When the unit-holders wanted to withdraw their money, Mr Young's fund could not meet their requests because it could not sell its investments except at a fraction of their cost price. If Hutton's thesis were correct, unit trust managers would be doing a service to their country if they behaved like Mr Young. (This is not to deny that the market economy has a role for venture capital funds, where investors cannot easily withdraw their funds and the money is trapped for a long period. But it is undoubtedly true that investors require a higher return from such funds than, say, unit trusts or a well-diversified, easily-realisable share portfolio held at a firm of stockbrokers.)

While the theory of the relationship between return and liquidity is in its infancy,[17] economics has in the last 30 years seen a burgeoning literature on financial development. One of its main conclusions is that, in their progress from low to high incomes per head, societies see the financial system growing faster than the economy as a whole.[18] It is indeed a salient feature of under-developed economies (such as those in Africa and parts of Asia) that their stock markets are not only badly-organised and illiquid, but that the ratio of their total capitalisation to national income is lower than in Britain and other industrial countries. The rate of return on capital is also typically much higher in under-developed economies than in rich countries belonging to the Organisation for Economic Cooperation and Development. Cross-country comparisons of this kind are compelling evidence of the benefits to societies of organised and liquid financial markets; they are far more convincing than Hutton's pseudo-historical conjectures about 'the seventeenth century', 'gentlemanly capitalists' and such like.

Hutton's most interesting new idea is therefore wrong. It is mistaken in terms of both economic theory and broad historical generalisation. Any plausible theory of portfolio choice has to include an inverse, not a positive, relationship between financial asset liquidity and the returns on physical capital, while the long sweep of history is from primitive, illiquid patterns of ownership to sophisticated, liquid financial markets, and from high to low returns on physical capital. The increase in asset liquidity and the decline in the return on capital take place in parallel.

But Hutton might be right about some aspects of Britain's financial institutions, even if the weaknesses are not quite what he thinks. For example, he would be correct that—if British investors require higher rates of return than investors elsewhere—British companies would have less capital per worker than their international competitors.[19] If Britain's financial institutions do seek unnecessarily high returns, this may not be due to their liquidity fetish, but it would still need to be discussed. In reviewing the evidence on the actual behaviour of the British financial system, four points need to be made.

Rates of Return on Capital

First, the rate of return on quoted equities needs to be distinguished from the rate of return on physical capital. Hutton fails to make this distinction; he takes it for granted that the impressive returns achieved by, for example, UK pension fund managers over the last 20 years translate into a demand for a high return on new investments in plant and buildings. This is not the case. The return on corporate equity and the return on physical capital are related, but they are not identical. Conceptually they differ for many reasons.

The rate of return on physical capital is, substantially, a technological and marketing matter; it is measured by the amount of profit (after meeting costs of production) in a particular period relative to the cost of the equipment or buildings. By contrast, the rate of return on quoted equities is a financial concept, which depends for example on pay-out ratios (i.e., the proportions of profit actually distributed to shareholders) and financial markets' valuations of prospective dividend streams over many periods (i.e., the change in the P/E multiples or dividend yield), as well as such mundane considerations as dealing costs. Moreover, the return on physical capital covers payments of interest to banks and bondholders, as well as the return to shareholders. Perhaps most fundamentally of all, equity investors are interested not just in a high rate of return on physical capital, but in a high rate of growth in profits and dividends. Companies (the tobacco giants) with a high return on capital but in a contracting industry may be less attractive to prospective shareholders than companies (in pharmaceuticals and electronics) with a low return on capital and exciting growth opportunities. In fact, equity investors routinely accept lower dividend yields on high-growth stocks than on average- or low-growth stocks, in the expectation that over time the returns on the different kinds of stock will be the same.

Secondly, because the rate of return on quoted equities is not the same as the rate of return on physical investment, Hutton's numbers need to be checked. Hutton is correct that British fund managers have over the last 20 years achieved spectacularly high returns on their investment securities. But it does not follow that UK industry has had a high rate of return on physical capital or, more crucially, that UK financial institutions have pressed for higher returns on new investments than their counterparts in other countries.

Low UK Rate of Return on Capital

The OECD has compiled statistics on 'the rate of return on capital in the business sector' for its member countries since 1970. They are summarized in Table 2 (p. 34). The message is very striking and totally contradicts Hutton's claims. *The rate of return on capital in the UK is the lowest of all the large OECD economies. In fact, since 1970 there has not been a single year when the rate of return on capital has been as high in the UK as in any other member of the G7 group of industrial countries.* This one fact effectively destroys Hutton's entire polemic about British companies being forced, but the City's reputed 'short-termism', to seek high returns. Indeed, Hutton's talk about the 'short-termist' City of London demanding 'insanely' high returns from industrial companies is shown to be preposterous.

Thirdly, Hutton has made a serious analytical mistake in using historical, after-the-event (*ex post*) figures for the return on financial investments as the basis for his claim that the real-world, before-the-event (*ex ante*) required return on physical capital in the UK is exceptionally high. Investors in stock markets achieve capital gains when the dividend yield on equities falls. Further, if everything else is equal, the lower the dividend yield on equities, the lower also is the return that the outside investors require on the physical capital. In other words, it is after periods of falling dividend yields and healthy capital gains (which will boost the *ex post* returns on equities) that the *ex ante* required return on physical capital is below normal. Conversely, it is after periods of rising dividend yields and poor capital gains (or losses) that the *ex ante* required return on physical capital is particularly high.

The real return on UK equities over the last 35 years has been about six or seven per cent a year. (The precise number depends on how the sums are done.)[20] But the 35 years splits neatly into two halves, the first before 1979 and the second afterwards. If a period of 15 to 20 years to 1979 is taken, the real return on UK equities was virtually nil; in the 17 years since 1979 it has been over 12 per cent a year. Hutton has protested that the sort of rate of return secured on equities since 1979 is excessive and sets an inappropriate target rate of return for companies. But this is misleading. Not only has Hutton himself been guilty of short-termism by neglecting to mention the longer-run 35-year record, but also he has failed to explain the dramatic contrast between the two halves of this 35-year period.

His problem is that the poor returns in the first half were partly due to a rise in the dividend yield. In other words, a long period of inadequate returns on financial securities was the result of a fall in investors' valuations of corporate equity, which boosted the return on physical capital that was acceptable to them. So the required return on physical capital was high in 1979. The strong returns on equities since 1979 reflect investors' improving valuation of corporate equity, which lowers the return that they need on physical capital. It follows that the required return on physical capital is substantially lower today than it was in 1979. A fair presumption is that the free-market, capitalist-minded policies of the post-1979 period, when companies have been increasingly subject to the alleged 'tyranny' of financial markets, have in fact expanded the range of capital projects that companies can undertake. Far from the City demanding higher company profitability today than in the corporatist era of, say, 1960 to 1979, the acceptable returns on equity are lower.

High UK Rate of Return on Physical Capital

Fourthly, both the rate of return on quoted equity and the rate of return on physical capital have to be distinguished from the rate of increase in the productivity of capital (i.e., the output per unit of capital). In some ways it is this final concept which is the fairest arbiter of the success of a nation's financial system. If Hutton were right that the UK's financial system has failed since 1979, the increase in capital productivity ought to have been lower than in other countries. The OECD has prepared some useful statistics, which are reproduced in Table 3 (p. 35). It turns out that, once again, Hutton's views are not just mistaken, but thoroughly wrong-headed. *The UK is the only major industrial country where the productivity of capital has increased since 1979.* The increase is particularly salient when compared with the fall in the UK's capital productivity in the corporatist 1960-79 period and with the miserable performance of Japan, so much lauded by Hutton for the supposed 'long-termism' of its financial sector. Japan has in fact over the last 20 years suffered the heaviest fall in capital productivity of any industrial nation.

It is not difficult to understand why Britain has been able so effectively to improve the management of its capital stock since 1979. Quite apart from the plethora of free-market reforms (curbs on trade union power, financial market liberalisation) which have done much for economic efficiency, there has been the enormous boost from privatisation. The evidence is now overwhelming that companies in public ownership from the late 1940s to the early 1980s were seriously inefficient, particularly in how they organised their capital stock. Privatisation has enabled their managements to achieve similar levels of output without extra investment and usually with much smaller workforces. Here lies a large part of the strong British showing in the international league table of capital productivity. If this is what Hutton's 'vandalisation' of the economy by the financial system has done, let's have more of it!

The Advantages of Liquidity and Short-termism

Hutton's critique of the British financial system is off-beam, even eccentric. He muddles concepts, ignores facts and rambles inconsistently between different arguments. It is a tribute to the eloquence and verve of his writing that Hutton has been able to craft a best-seller from such ingredients. Nevertheless, an interesting new topic is trying to escape from all the babble of *The State We're In*, namely the nature of the relationship between financial market liquidity and asset returns.

Hutton says that liquidity is bad, because it raises the required return on capital. Actually, he has got the argument the wrong way round. Liquidity is good because it reduces the required return on capital. Indeed, one of the main social benefits from secondary market financial activity is that, because it is associated with a lower return on capital, it expands a nation's equilibrium capital stock and thereby increases living standards. Economists are only beginning to theorize in this area, but the very-long-run evidence of history confirms the idea. A good general rule is that 'liquid financial markets and banking systems grow faster than national income, as incomes per head increase'. Secondary market activity is not parasitic and wasteful, but an integral part of market capitalism.

Shareholders' ability to buy and sell corporate equity is particularly helpful in ensuring that the capital stock is used efficiently; it may therefore be crucial in explaining why capitalism, whose key institutions were pioneered in Britain, has triumphed against rival systems of property ownership in the last 300 years. These institutions, both in Britain and elsewhere, may be characterised by 'short-termism' in the sense defined by Hutton. In other words, they may give investors the ability to reverse decisions quickly, easily and cheaply in organised capital markets. But, if that is what short-termism means, it is a virtue—not a vice—of Western market economies. It is part of the explanation for their formidable efficiency in accumulating and managing capital. Hutton is right that since 1979 Britain has become more capitalist, with formerly nationalised assets coming under private ownership and the financial system operating more freely than before. Although it may come as a shock to him, the living standards of the British people have improved as a result.

Table 1 Returns on equities and cash, 1945-95

Table shows real returns (i.e., after adjustment for retail prices), % p.a. averages of five-year periods. There has been only one five-year period, out of the last 11, in which cash has beaten equities.

Five years to	Ind. Ord. share index	3-month Treasury bills (i.e., cash for large financial institutions)
1945	11.4	-2.6
1950	2.2	-3.4
1955	11.4	-2.2
1960	17.2	2.1
1965	3.7	1.4
1970	5.8	2.0
1975	-7.9	-4.1
1980	6.8	-2.9
1985	16.6	3.5
1990	9.4	5.1
1995	8.8	3.7
Average of all 11 five-year periods	7.8	0.2

Source: Bacon & Woodrow, reproduced in NTC Publications *Pension Pocket Book 1997*

Table 2 The return on capital in the leading OECD economies

Table shows "rate of return on capital in the business sector", % p.a.

	Average for: 1970-78	1979-87	1988-87
USA	15.3	15.2	17.5
Japan	18.3	14.0	14.7
Germany	11.8	11.0	12.8
France	12.7	11.2	14.6
Italy	11.6	13.2	15.1
UK	10.2	9.4	10.6
Canada	14.8	18.2	18.4
G7 as a whole	14.7	13.8	15.7

Souce: OECD *Economic Outlook*, December 1996, p.A28.

Table 3 The rate of change in capital productivity

Table shows increase in output per unit of capital, % p.a., based on a calculation for "total factor productivity". For details, see source. The UK was the only member of the G7 where productivity per unit of capital increased from 1979 to 1995.

	Average for: 1960-73	1973-79	1979-95
USA	2.3	-0.2	-0.2
Japan	-3.3	-3.7	-2.1
Germany	-1.4	-1.0	-0.6
France	0.6	-1.0	-0.6
Italy	0.4	0.3	-0.9
UK	-0.3	-1.5	0.5
Canada	0.2	-1.0	-2.4
G7 as a whole	0.3	-1.1	-0.7

Souce: OECD *Economic Outlook*, December 1996, p.A68.

The gap in valuations between quoted and unquoted companies

The chart below is taken from BDO Stoy Hayward's *Private Company Price Index*, issue 3, 1996. The top line is the P/E ratio for the *Financial Times* non-financials shares index; the bottom line is the P/E ratio for private companies.

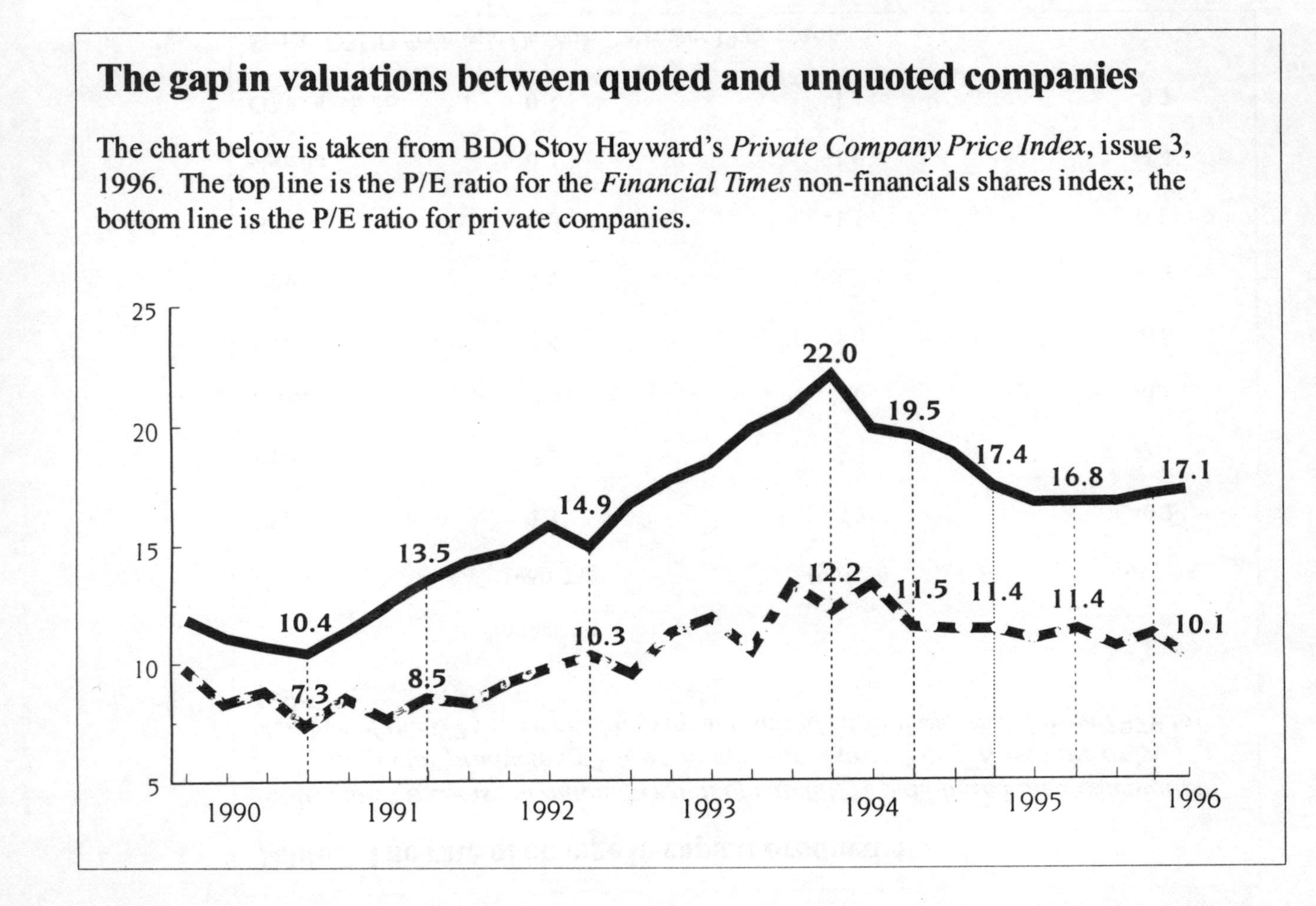

Will Hutton and Welfare Reform

David G. Green

Will Hutton's main hope for the welfare state is to preserve as much as possible of it whilst permitting different levels of payment and correspondingly different levels of service.[1] He argues that the NHS should be based on tiered contributions to allow improved services for 'non-life-threatening' treatments, presumably to include private rooms and better hospital amenities.[2] Unemployment benefit, too, would be reformed so that higher contributions would lead to higher benefits.[3] In education, there would be no payment, but the state system should include grammar schools and permit streaming within comprehensives.[4]

His reasoning is that the middle class pays the tax for the welfare state and they need to 'get enough out of the system directly' to make them support it.[5] He knows that he is criticised for 'nationalising inequality', but considers it necessary because 'by incorporating inequality into the public domain at least it is contained and managed'.[6] Without streaming and grammar schools under the state system, for example, there would be a 'middle-class exodus'.[7]

Hutton's View of the Market

His wider criticism is that since 1979 the market has been 'the sole organising principle of economy and society'. He continues:

> The financial and employment systems have been deregulated, while the government has attempted to design the welfare and tax system so as to maximise the rewards for 'enterprise' and the penalties for 'idleness'. Wherever possible—from the National Health Service to the provision of pensions—market forces have been promoted and state intervention rolled back.[8]

The intrusion of the market, he says, has destroyed social cohesion, caused family breakdown, bad parenting, and rising crime.[9] Moreover:

> The collapse of social cohesion that comes when the market is allowed to rip through society has produced a fall in the growth rate; marginalisation, deprivation and exclusion have proved economically irrational.[10]

He deploys a very narrow view of 'the market', as a theory that reduces everything to cash:

> The controlling idea is that the human being is a trader, constantly weighing up the advantages and disadvantages of various courses of action. And because the essence of a market is that courses of action have a price tag, every act can be reduced to an economic calculus weighing up the costs and benefits of each action.[11]

Hutton insists that, contrary to the claims of the 'new right':

> Men and women are social animals, but with conflicting demands and passions. They seek association with each other and value the esteem of others; they desire health and autonomy. They thrive on the stimulus of competition, they recognise the value of co-operation, the importance of security and the need for boundaries to individual action. They seek happiness and a good quality of life, but these are not absolutes—they are substantially influenced by culture and social mores.[12]

These passages contain a number of mistaken assumptions.

First, that under Thatcherism the market became the sole organising principle of society.

Second, that free marketeers do not care about social cohesion or 'community' but reduce everything to a cash nexus.

Third, that several serious social problems that have come to public attention since 1979 were the result of 'the market'.

The Market as the Sole Organising Principle of Society

His first claim is that the market has become the sole organising principle of society. However, Hutton does not entertain the possibility that Thatcherism as a political movement drew on a variety of intellectual influences of which the 'market' was only one. For example, the Tories remained strongly paternalistic in their attitude to the welfare state, and came under heavy criticism from the market-oriented think tanks for doing so. They made no serious effort to reform welfare and have consistently dodged difficult issues, hence the huge increase in social security spending since 1979. Spending on social security alone increased by about 62 per cent in real terms between 1981/82 and

1995/96.[13] In other words, 'the market' was not the *sole* organising principle, but one of several.

Not only did Thatcherism draw on several intellectual traditions, but the 'new right' itself was not monolithic. As a label it covers the anarcho-libertarianism of Ayn Rand and David Friedman, the constitutional liberalism of James Buchanan, the hard-boiled economism of Gary Becker, and the cultural or evolutionary liberalism of Hayek.

Social Cohesion

His second claim is that the new right does not care about social cohesion.

All political philosophies inevitably make assumptions about the human condition and, according to Hutton, we are 'social animals'. However, he then goes on to make a false contrast. In his view, we can either see ourselves as united in pursuit of a common purpose, or as 'isolated individuals'. That is, we can view ourselves as part of a team with a shared objective, or as individuals linked only by economic calculation.

Hutton's assumptions about the human condition lead to a particular view of government. In his view, a society is a team with the government as the leader. He makes no secret of his mistrust of individual choice and responsibility. We 'cannot be relied upon to make judgements that are rational'; rationality is 'too difficult for human beings to cope with', he says.[14] And like all socialist theories, his low view of the rank and file is matched by a high regard for the capabilities of the leaders, whose task is to manage and direct lives.

Again he deploys a false contrast: the only alternative to 'unity in pursuit of a common purpose' is the minimal state:

> Today's New Right do no more than repeat the ancestral warnings of the laissez-faire economists over the last two centuries: interfere in the operation of the market at your peril; inequality is the price we pay for efficiency; liberty of contract is an indivisible principle; the poor will always be with us; help is self-defeating.[15]

How does Hutton's caricature compare with what the classical liberals actually said? Adam Smith's theory of human nature was, not that the most powerful impulse was self-interest, but rather the inclination to seek the approval of others. We have, he argued, a built-in moral sense based on this search for approval.

There were two main 'tribunals'. The first was based on the desire for 'actual praise' and the avoidance of 'actual blame'; and the second, the desire for 'praiseworthiness' and to avoid 'blameworthiness'. People at their best, said Smith, like to receive praise which is genuinely deserved.

Smith is best known for *The Wealth of Nations*, but *The Theory of Moral Sentiments* was his first book and was originally published in 1759. It was revised constantly during his lifetime. There were six editions of the book and the final edition of 1790 was published only a year before his death. The alterations made to successive editions were substantial, whereas *The Wealth of Nations* underwent comparatively minor revision. A plain and unbiased reading of *The Theory of Moral Sentiments* reveals that Smith understood a free society, not as a jungle held together by self-interest, but as a moral association of people united by their attachment to shared laws and morals, all upheld during the course of ordinary day-to-day activity.

Thus, for the Adam-Smith liberal, a society should not be conceived as a team of followers under leadership, but as an association united by commitment to common rules. There is a sense of community. It is based on shared morals, acceptance of laws applying equally to all, and everyone doing their bit to uphold the culture by personal example. Adam-Smith liberalism is not a celebration of atomistic individualism.

Nor, contrary to Hutton's claim, was every action of government seen as an infringement of liberty. Hutton quotes Spencer,[16] whose animosity to government was extreme, but he is outside the main tradition of liberalism that can be traced from Adam Smith to Hayek.

Hayek frequently took pains to explain that he did not defend *laissez faire*:

> Not Locke, nor Hume, nor Smith, nor Burke, could ever have argued, as Bentham did, that 'every law is an evil for every law is an infraction of liberty'. Their argument was never a complete *laissez-faire* argument ... They knew better than most of their later critics that it was not some sort of magic but the evolution of 'well-constructed institutions' ... that had successfully channelled individual efforts to socially beneficial aims. In fact, their argument was never anti-state as such, or anarchistic, which is the logical outcome of the rationalistic *laissez-faire* doctrine; it was an argument that accounted both for the proper functions of the state and for the limits of state action.[17]

The Adam-Smith liberals were not anti-government. They believed that government had important but limited duties. Adam Smith had no doubts that freedom depended on law. The factor which contributed above all to prosperity was, he said:

> that equal and impartial administration of justice which renders the rights of the meanest British subject respectable to the greatest, and which, by securing to every man the fruits of his own industry, gives the greatest and most effectual encouragement to every sort of industry.[18]

Disentangling Cause and Effect

Hutton explains events since 1979 as the result of 'the market'. But 'the market' has not been the main, let alone the only, cause of events. Among the ruling doctrines from World War Two until 1979 was 'economic collectivism'. It was abandoned after 1979, first by Thatcher governments and later by New Labour. But in addition to the attack on capitalist economics there was also an assault on the culture of capitalism, that is on the 'bourgeois values' that sustain it. This attack still continues and is focussed on two particular ideas: (i) education as the transmission of a culture, or an ideal way of living, from generation to generation; and (ii) the traditional family based on marriage. What both 'education as cultural transmission' and 'the family' have in common is that they hold up standards or ideals for the young to judge themselves by. That is, in the view of critics, they are concerned with guilt, stereotypes, 'social control' or repression.

Until the late 1970s 'the left' advocated this combination of economic collectivism and cultural nihilism, with three main targets in mind: private property, the bourgeois family, and education as the transmission of culture. In attacking these institutions, they struck at the main pillars of a free society. From 1979, economic collectivism was defeated, but not cultural nihilism.

Hutton could have attacked the Tories for their failure to tackle these issues, as others on the left have done, including the *Observer* columnist Melanie Phillips[19] and Norman Dennis, not to mention IEA authors such as Patricia Morgan. Instead, Hutton chose to blame family breakdown and related problems on 'the market', diverting his gaze from the real causes.

He could with justice have criticised some libertarian intellectuals—adherents of hard-boiled economism—for failing to overcome their own ambiguity about morals. There was in the 1980s an agreement between some free-marketeers and some economic collectivists that individual release from moral restraints was desirable. Both felt it was 'authoritarian' to assert any view of right or wrong and some economists continue to write as if they believe that 'the market' supplies its own morality. They rightly point out that competition compared with monopoly increases the chances that wrongdoers will be found out and, therefore, encourages good conduct, but increased visibility is not enough on its own. Human virtues, excellence of character, belief in reasonable standards of right and wrong, all have to be upheld by institutions that are outside any system of market transactions. As one Adam-Smith liberal put it:

> The market, competition, and the play of supply and demand do not create these ethical reserves; they presuppose them and consume them. These reserves have to come from outside the market ... Self-discipline, a sense of justice, honesty, fairness, chivalry, moderation, public spirit, respect for human dignity, firm ethical norms—all of these are things which people must possess before they go to market and compete with each other. These are the indispensable supports which preserve both market and competition from degeneration.[20]

The underlying assumption of hard-boiled economism is that freedom is the absence of all outside restraint or pressure, but as Hayek showed, this view confuses freedom with power. Hutton does not criticise this view because he appears also to subscribe to what might be called the get-out-of-my-face theory of freedom.

He bases his arguments on a theory of human nature which gives high prominence to self-interest narrowly defined. The middle class, he says, is out for what it can get; socialists should recognise this fact and devise systems that preserve as much of the welfare state as possible while keeping the middle class 'on board'. Like all socialist schemes, his world is made up of individuals who are being manipulated from the outside by a 'system designer'. The aim of the education system is to 'imbue the middle class with a sense of their common citizenship, whilst recognising their impulse for self-advancement'.[21] The aim of health reform is to give the middle class a 'vested interest' in the entire system: 'it opts in rather than opts out, thus underpinning universality and common purpose rather than privatisation and social fragmentation'.[22]

The manner in which he criticises the Tory reform of the welfare state is also weak. He claims that they have reformed it to conform to market dogma and that the social problems of the 1990s, including family breakdown, rising crime and benefit dependency are the result of these 'market' reforms. Hutton appears to believe that there is a causal connection between the ideas of 'new-right' intellectuals like Hayek and Friedman—via the instrument of Thatcherite policies—and the social problems of the 1990s. His first difficulty has already been touched upon, namely that the 'new right' did not all take the same view (even Hayek and Friedman, for example, disagreed so strongly about monetary policy that they avoided discussing the topic). But more importantly, Thatcher governments, far from pursuing the policies advocated by the new right, maintained and defended policies that before 1979 had been universally called 'socialism'.

Hutton would have been closer to the truth if he had criticised the Tories for their lack of consistency. If they had rigidly adhered to 'new-right' dogma they would have privatised the welfare state. In reality they did nothing of the sort.

What Will Hutton Should Have Said

If his view had not been distorted by partisan loyalty, he could have advanced a more accurate criticism of Tory welfare policies. He could have said that they deployed a narrow and stunted view of 'the market' which feebly imitated the ideas of Adam-Smith liberalism.

The Tories saw themselves as managers of the nation, designing incentives to bring about desired outcomes. We may call their view 'mechanical' or 'administrative' economism. Individuals are viewed as self-interested and the political challenge is to design the appropriate incentives. Their health reforms provide a good example. The internal market is a pale imitation of the real thing. In education, policies were based on central direction, particularly by means of the national curriculum, and the language of parental choice was used mostly as rhetoric.

Hutton did not advance this line of criticism because he shares many of the Tories assumptions. His world, too, is made up of self-interested individuals who are being manipulated by a system designer. This attitude has made it difficult for him to understand that his criticisms do not apply to the whole classical-liberal heritage, but only to aspects of the peculiar philosophical mix that has influenced government policy since 1979.

For the Adam-Smith liberal, the basic building block is not self-interest, but character. 'Self-interest' implies a person with a given set of personal preferences; 'character' implies an individual capable of self-improvement and being guided by a sense of duty to others. Dispositions such as these are fostered by practice rather than precept, and consequently depend for their transmission from generation to generation on primary groups, such as the family and voluntary associations. It follows that the viability of these groups is of the utmost importance, and the challenge for the Adam-Smith liberal is to maintain them in good order. As the powers of government have expanded this century, it has tended to undermine some of these intermediate associations, by assuming the responsibilities they previously took on. Hutton's misunderstandings have prevented him from seeing this reality. When he raises moral issues he is pronouncing judgement on the rights and wrongs of political decisions. There is no sign that he has understood the importance for liberty of preserving the good health of civil society. He makes no distinction between 'the community' and the political system. Yet, it is through the elemental groups that make up the community that morals are upheld—through personal example rather than preaching.

The ideal of Adam-Smith liberalism is not to create a 'market' in the narrow sense in which the term is mostly used, namely commercial activity. It is the renewal of civil society, a term which includes commercial activity but which is far wider, embracing human co-operation motivated by mutual and charitable ideals as well as commercial objectives. I turn now to specific issues, in the hope of explaining more fully the importance of renewing civil society.

Welfare Dependency and Assisting the Poor

Hutton implies that the 'new right' has the harsh attitude towards the poor that he associates with 19th century *laissez faire.* According to Hutton, the new right regards inequality as positively desirable. Moreover: 'There needs to be fear and greed in the system to make it tick.'[23] But as we shall see, no positive value is attached to inequality, let alone fear.

We can understand how Hutton's approach differs from Adam-Smith liberalism by contrasting the views of protagonists in the nineteenth-century welfare debate. Modern historians have tended to divide them into two groups: the harsh and the kind. But this was not how it was seen at the time. The Adam-Smith liberals were in no doubt about the importance of kindness, for them the issue was how to be kind without doing more harm than good.

I will take as an example Helen Bosanquet, the main author of the majority report of the Royal Commission on the Poor Laws of 1909. She was emphatic that no one should be neglected:

> no greater blow could be struck at the feeling of unity which holds a community together than that a part of it should be allowed to perish for want while another part could have assisted and did not.[24]

But, she argues, 'a community owes much more to its members than the mere maintenance of life'. Indeed, it is because efforts to assist the poor aim so low that such deplorable results have been achieved.[25]

No person can be raised merely by giving money, because once self-respect is lost, the economic results are out of all proportion to the size of the subsidy.[26] To destroy a man's interest in self-maintenance destroys a 'guiding force'; it is 'moral murder'.[27] True respect involves making demands, because we cannot grow as people without a struggle to overcome difficulties. A civilisation is best understood as an ideal way of living. As such, it is an inheritance waiting for all, but each must exert himself to benefit from it:

> To deprive an individual human being ... of the necessity ... of planning his life for himself, is to deprive him of his natural power of 'progressive development'.[28]

When a life of dependency is chosen it also has practical consequences. People neglect relationships that would allow them to ask for help: they allow friendships to wither, or neglect family ties, or do not join organisations that would lend a helping hand.[29] For this reason, thoughtless help involving the giving of money without understanding can make matters worse.

Helen Bosanquet did not apply her argument only to the poor:

> To exempt any class, whether on the score of their poverty or their wealth, their toil or their idleness, from the claims to which the highest part of our nature responds, is *ipso facto*, to place them

outside the pale of humanity, and to deliberately throw aside the most powerful instrument for their redemption.[30]

Adam-Smith liberals believed that the purpose of welfare measures was to ensure that all should have the prospect of making an independent contribution. Help should, therefore, be aimed at restoring independence. When it does the opposite, it has failed. The restoration of independence was about identifying the people who could benefit from face-to-face assistance and ensuring that they get it, including those who needed to be criticised for their own good. No less important, efforts to help the less fortunate brought people together. To reinvigorate civil society constant effort was required to build and to rebuild the social fabric by extending opportunities to serve others and not looking to public officials to discharge important functions.

Mrs Bosanquet directed her fire, as much against the unwise public authorities as against private charities who also increased welfare dependency. By the late 1860s it had become obvious that indiscriminate charity could do as much harm as indiscriminate benefit.[31] A contrast began to be made between charity that strengthened independence and charity that demoralised. In particular, the charity of some churches had often been impulsive and sentimental, reflected especially in its reluctance to exercise critical judgement.

Will Hutton's approach resembles that of the sentimental vicars or lady bountifuls who saw in the poor a benighted group who must be helped—but they helped without understanding, as he does.

Helen Bosanquet was scathing about 19th century contemporaries who held Hutton's views:

> The very people who insist most upon the duty of Society with a big S towards its members, are most blind to the significance of the duties of the society which is composed of actual concrete individuals—the man's neighbours and relations.[32]

In the name of 'society' such people destroyed the real communities that were already there.

Octavia Hill, another nineteenth-century liberal champion of the poor, also compared 'unthinking' church charity with the 'befriending' charity based on personal knowledge and faith in potential for improvement:

> The ideal the poor form for themselves is low, and the rich support them in it. The rich, on the other hand, while they are continually

> coming forward more and more to help the poor, are thoroughly cowardly about telling them any truth that is unpalatable, and know too little of them to meet them really as friends, and learn to be natural and brave with them. We have great relief funds and little manly friendship, idleness above and below, and an admiration for what is pleasant which degrades all life. This temper makes work difficult, and sometimes fills one with wondering awe about the future of rich and poor.[33]

The dole charities, as the philanthropic bodies that gave money and little else were called, had no faith in the potential of poor individuals for change. Their philosophy was undemanding, both of the people being helped and those giving aid—perhaps that was its appeal. When the state took increasing responsibility for the work of charities, it did not learn these lessons. Indeed, during the late nineteenth and early twentieth centuries many of those involved in dole charities transferred their allegiance from church to the state.

These are the issues raised by modern social security. Others on the left have seen this, not least Frank Field. Hutton's preoccupation with equality of outcome, and his desire to blame 'the market' distracted him from the real problems. The challenge in social security reform is not to promote equality of outcome, but to encourage excellence of character and to restore resilience to the institutions of civil society.

Health

Hutton's criticisms of 'the market' approach to the NHS have more credibility than his views on social security. The Thatcher reforms of 1990 used the 'market' language of incentives, prices and 'money following patients', but the main thrust was to increase the power of managers at the expense of doctors in order to improve efficiency. The system continued to be centrally directed with market-like incentives deployed as management tools.

However, Hutton's animosity to 'the market' as such prevents him from making a distinction between a policy partially based on market elements and a full-fledged competitive system. The 'internal market' resembles a 'defence industry procurement' model of competition in which, either a short-list of suppliers submit tenders, or a government agency 'negotiates' with a contractor. It produces very different results from a 'consumer sovereignty' model of competition in which paying customers choose among alternatives.

The internal market, even in economic terms, does not produce the benefits of a competitive market. Prices serve at least two useful purposes. First, they allow consumers to make a more informed judgement between the various goods and services available, from foreign holidays to the education of children. Under a 'free' system, which in practice means one financed by compulsion, the consumer has no way of comparing the cost of health care with other desirable things. The compulsion removes responsibility for choice. Second, prices send signals to suppliers about demand, enabling them to judge the standard of care people expect and how many hospitals to build or medical personnel to train. Experience since 1948 suggests that government planning of facilities causes rationing. The 'prices' under the internal market do not empower consumers; they serve as inadequate guides to investment; and tend to concentrate the provider's attention on costs rather than quality.

Moreover, in Hayek's analogy, a truly competitive market is a process of 'discovery'. By allowing all comers to try their hand at their own risk, we make three types of discovery: which *people* are successful in meeting consumer preferences, which *products or services* are wanted, and which *prices* customers will pay.

Hutton could have lambasted the Tories, not only for their deficient understanding, but also for failing to tackle the real problems of the NHS. It has two main weaknesses. First, because it is government financed, global budgets have been set. The result has been rationing, including the withholding of life-saving treatment. Second, because it is a public-sector monopoly, the providers have no real incentive to serve consumers. Hutton did not attack these faults because he too wants public-sector monopoly and global budgets. Instead of proposing a solution that would put everyone, rich or poor, in a stronger position, he argues in favour of *one* system for all. But, his desire for 'inclusion' is a demand for continued public-sector monopoly and compulsory finance. His only concession is to urge fellow socialists to be more pragmatic about preserving middle-class commitment to public-sector monopoly. For this reason, he is willing to permit additional payments for non-essential extras, so long as there is *one* system. He displays no awareness that there can be universal access without public-sector monopoly.

He also shows no awareness of the arguments advanced by Adam-Smith liberals who urge, not merely a free market, let alone an 'internal market', but the restoration of civil society. Some economists have given the impression that the only approved motivation is commercial, a mistake criticised by Hayek, who drew attention to the importance of a third, independent, sector which is neither 'government' nor 'commerce'.[34] No less important, non-commercial motivation is possibly more relevant in health care than in any other sphere. Before 1948, the majority of acute hospital admissions were to voluntary hospitals and before national insurance in 1911, primary care was largely organised on mutual principles.[35] Commercial activity played only a small part.

The impressive record of the voluntary hospitals has a double significance. They had not only been providing a steadily improving service for decades by the time they were nationalised, but also provided a focal point for people of good will. Individuals could help as hospital visitors, as fund raisers, by giving blood, or in providing 'extras' like refreshments or books for patients to read. The hospitals were outlets for all manner of human decencies. Nationalisation did not wholly eradicate this tradition, but it did cause a significant reduction.

A remedy consistent with Adam-Smith liberalism would have two main elements. First, the power of the state would be used, not to preserve public-sector monopoly, but to guarantee access to all whether rich or poor, whilst leaving most people free to choose their own health insurer. And second, hospitals would be re-voluntarised, not only to create competition, but to reinvigorate civil society. Another IEA paper proposes how this might be accomplished.[36]

Because the Tory government was interested primarily in efficiency, and not in empowering the consumer, it imposed an internal market instead of renewing civil society. Hutton's proposals also fail to empower consumers.

Education

Because his book is an attack on 'the market' he is inclined to brand the education reforms with the label 'market'. But as in health policy, the Conservatives preserved public-sector monopoly more or less intact and pursued a strategy which could just as easily be called 'socialist'. They did decentralise school budgets, they did introduce city technology colleges, and they did create grant-maintained schools, and each measure slightly weakened the grip of the central state. However, these small gains were counterbalanced by the imposition of the highly centralised national curriculum.

Like the Tories, Hutton, is a centralist who insists that there must be *one* system in which all are included. Without this 'inclusion' there can be no social cohesion, he says. And once more, in the name of society, he ends by destroying real communities, for schools like hospitals can be a powerful focus for community spirit in each locality.

His concern for 'inclusion' is, in practice, a rationale for public-sector monopoly. His 'inclusion' means forcing people to pay for a service, whether they believe it to be good or bad. It puts them in a weak position. But Hutton does not seem to understand that to undermine the authority of parents in education is especially harmful. Schools do not only teach academic knowledge or particular skills, but prepare children for adulthood, and this task is best accomplished when parents and schools work hand in hand. For schools and parents to share the same ethos, it is of fundamental importance that every school should be a chosen school. And to ensure that the balance of power does not favour the school, then each should rely on parents for payment, for unless schools depend on parents for their income, the bargaining power of parents will be weakened.

Here there is an important role for the state to ensure that no child goes without education. Many on 'the left', whose principal concern is that the poor should enjoy access, have argued in favour of a voucher scheme to empower consumers. Professor Le Grand, for instance, favours vouchers, so long as bigger payments are made to the less well off.[37]

Once more, Hutton's approach amounts to the preservation of public-sector monopoly, whilst making sufficient concessions to the middle class to maintain its support. His pre-occupation with 'inclusion'—his word for public-sector monopoly—has blinded him to the real problems.

Among the most powerful arguments against public-sector monopoly is that concentrated power may be captured by the wrong people. The lesson of post-war education is surely that monopoly power in education has, indeed, been captured by the wrong people. The education system has been a prime target of elements seeking to undermine 'bourgeois society'. The Tories after 1979 sought to turn the tide by using the power of the state to enforce their own view, particularly by means of the national curriculum.

If they had been more under the influence of Adam-Smith liberalism, and less guided by Tory paternalism, they would have understood that diverse ownership and competition are preferable because they avoid concentrated power. In the absence of centrally concentrated power, errors are more likely to occur on a smaller scale and, because diversity facilitates comparison, more likely to be speedily identified and corrected. Summerhill, for instance, was a celebrated experiment of the 1960s in 'laid back' schooling whose mistakes only affected a few people. If the state had enforced such an experiment across the country, the cost would have been huge. Indeed, when education was dominated by the anti-achievement ethos of the 1960s and 1970s it did have a harmful and lasting impact on millions of children.

A remedy compatible with Adam Smith liberalism would be to ensure access for all through education vouchers and to reinvigorate civil society by removing schools from the political control of local authorities to the ownership of charitable trusts comprising representatives of the local community.

Conclusions

Will Hutton misunderstands the tradition of freedom to which classical liberals belong. He thinks it is about being against government.

He not only misunderstands the ideal of liberty but also reveals no awareness of the institutions that emerged before the welfare state under the impact of 'market' doctrine. In health care the favoured institution was not the for-profit hospital but the voluntary hospital run by a charitable trust; in social security it was not 'fear and greed', nor even the poor law, but mutual aid and 'befriending' charity; and in education it was not the for-profit school, but local schools run by charitable trusts. The 'public schools' for the rich so despised by Hutton had their place, but so too did the Ragged Schools, the grammar schools open to all, the elementary schools and the Sunday schools, all committed to ensuring that every child was given a good start in life.

Hutton seems to think that cohesion can only be brought about by government. In truth, government has diminished cohesion by displacing the organisations that foster it. Hutton has no conception of civil society or 'community' as distinct from the state. He does not see the value of strong voluntary associations in protecting against concentrations of political power, in part because he has his own plans for the use of concentrated political power. He does not appear to see the value of fostering good character through voluntary co-operation with others. And he does not see that restoring welfare to civil society would foster cohesion based on mutual respect. Will Hutton speaks of the importance of 'inclusion', but fails to see that there can be universality without monopoly.[38]

Though Hutton resents the charge that he defends the old socialism—and it is true that he does not advocate the old supply-side socialism—on health, education and welfare he remains a 'system-design' socialist who has not yet understood that the classical-liberal welfare ideal is not the creation of a 'market' but the reinvigoration of civil society.

Stakeholding in the High Street

Sir Stanley Kalms

A basic requirement of any political essay is that the reader should be able to recognise the facts and empathise with the arguments, before coming to an independent conclusion. Will Hutton's piece fails to clear these hurdles. His woeful polemic lacks grass-roots foundations and is clearly not influenced either by fact, or by intercourse with the wider business community.

Needing compensatory models for his repudiation of Britain, he has, extraordinarily, chosen Germany and by implication France. It's worth mentioning that his chosen models are in a great economic mess.

All economic systems have flaws—they are after all a reflection of the defects of *homo sapiens*. The question is whether bolting on something called stakeholding could bring added social and economic value to the nation. Let's view stakeholding through the eyes of a British industrialist.

'Product markets are fiercely competitive but producers build up long-term relations of trust with their suppliers, financiers and work-forces' (p. 3). That's Hutton describing East Asian capitalism. It could equally be a description of the current situation in this country. Dixons and most other successful British businesses already have excellent relationships with their investors, suppliers, employees and customers. But such relationships are and should remain voluntary. Time after time Hutton chooses to turn a blind eye to UK successes because to highlight them would destroy the case for imposing a stakeholding system in Britain. British retailing, to name but one sector, is amongst the best in the world by almost every criteria—on profitability, investment, service to the customer (particularly compared to Germany), on efficient use of labour, and on several other key comparisons.

Hutton is wrong in claiming that 'long-term relations of trust' do not exist in Britain's economic supply chain. The fact is they do, and they negate the need for his stakeholding model. Hutton envisages state interference in the work of the financial institutions, stakeholder representation on company boards and a new Companies Act. Rather than leaving companies free to take a pragmatic, realistic approach, Hutton demands an enforceable 'duty of care': in other words a legislative straitjacket.

Laying down hard and fast rules for business relationships would never work. What, precisely, would Dixons' duties of care be? First, to the supplier. Would we be required to enter into indefinite contracts to buy or sell whatever is produced, or guarantee a place on the shelves of our stores? How would we conduct price negotiations when a decision to buy had already been prescribed? Dixons has more suppliers than it needs in most product groups. Would we have to spread our purchases evenly, or adhere to a more bureaucratic formula? Would we be forbidden to play one supplier off against another to get better prices? Must we forfeit the right to negotiate the best deal and instead allow suppliers to set our terms?

Already the follies of stakeholding are apparent and we have not yet come to the critical issue—the consumer, the ultimate decision maker. What happens if, after all the cosy incestuous deals are done, and our 'duty of care' has been invoked, the customer says 'no' and refuses to buy? In the real world the retailer is not the selector, only the intermediary.

How do we define a 'duty of care' to consumers? Fixed margins, co-operative style rebates? In a market economy, the consumer gains far more than he ever would in a regulated stakeholder society. Today's consumer enjoys ever higher standards of service and immensely competitive prices. Whoever else is being squeezed in the economy, consumers have truly never had it so good.

Employees are also caught in the web of Hutton's stakeholder theory, and here his grasp on reality becomes very tenuous. The nature of employer/employee relationships cannot be codified by the abstract theorist. Such relationships constitute the heart and soul of the business, the vital asset. No room here for academic pontificating. Companies already have a range of legal obligations to employees and, equally, employees themselves have obligations to the company: working conditions, respect, opportunity, progressive increases, shared risk and reward. But what this relationship must not become is a tight, inward, self-protecting circle against the vicissitudes of the market. It is the company's responsibility to be careful with the hirings and not to over-react to short-term situations. But it is not, and never could be, possible to guarantee jobs for life. In any case such a guarantee would be undesirable for employers and employees: mobility is a two-way privilege.

Hutton writes of the necessity of legislation to enforce all his wondrous concepts. He says that we must accept regulation and intervention in the new order. It is proposed that capital investment goes through an entirely new evaluation hoop, with the traditional return on capital criteria being dismissed as unaccountable finance.

All this leads to the conclusion that Hutton would like to see government control all economic life, both macro and micro. The real stakeholder would be the state. Under the innocuous-sounding label of stakeholding lurks an ill thought-out and dangerous philosophy of collectivism. Hutton may deny this but the facts speak for themselves.

Hutton's theories bear a disquieting resemblance to the pre-Yeltsin system that prevailed in Russia. He fails to recognise a fundamental law of economics: much of the strength and dynamism of the market economy system, the buyer/seller relationship, is driven by one thing—a degree of healthy uncertainty, and the knowledge that across the supply chain no relationship can simply be taken for granted. The need to continually improve in quality, design and price, to seek new markets and discard less profitable ones, is the irrefutable core of capitalism. Reduce uncertainty and in marches complacency, and this country had a bellyful of that from the old nationalised industries.

It is surely misleading for Hutton to claim that his theories are a definitive synthesis of the great liberal tradition. When we subject his views to close examination they are shown to be incorrect.

Regrettably, the Labour Party sees political opportunity in the issue. At one stage Tony Blair seized on Hutton's critique as the 'big idea' to help him to Number 10. The urgent task for business is to expose Hutton's contentions for the menace they really are.

Market Theory, Competition and the Stakeholder Society

Martin Ricketts

Introduction

Will Hutton's book *The State We're In* represents a comprehensive indictment of British institutions. This comment addresses two main issues. The first is theoretical. Hutton confuses 'free market economics' with support for a particular type of classical contracting. In fact it is quite possible to support market processes whilst being highly critical (like Hutton himself) of some of the contexts into which 'contracts' have been introduced in recent years.

The second issue concerns Hutton's support for Japanese and German models of corporate governance. Here he greatly underestimates the potential hazards of these systems and in particular the ability of the managerial élite to ignore the interests of savers.

Free Market Theory

Hutton believes in the power of ideas. One idea he thinks has been especially powerful and pernicious is that of the self regulating market economy. The doctrines of free market economics are 'bizarre' and their theoretical foundations 'embarrassingly flimsy' (p. 7). The worst error, writes Hutton, is to believe in a general competitive equilibrium, a theoretical edifice which requires abstractions such as complete markets and an 'auctioneer'. Departures from these arcane and unrealistic conditions wreck the whole free market model. It is now 'proved to be nonsense. It does not hold in theory. It is not true'.[1] Yet it has been the underlying intellectual foundation for the programmes of successive Conservative administrations—the altar upon which British industry has been sacrificed. The market 'overrides culture and institutions'[2] dissolves long standing social links and leads to short-termism and moral bankruptcy.

To attack Walrasian general equilibrium theory as a means of discrediting the important tenets of 'free market economics' is to fall into error and to misunderstand the entire intellectual history of these debates since around 1930. Hutton's explanation of the problems of Walrasian theory—the abstraction from any meaningful notion of the passage of time, the huge informational requirements, the existence of true uncertainty—will be disorientating for those who may have spent much of their professional lives making the same points in defence of a truly market agenda. Hutton seems utterly oblivious of the fact that the case for 'free markets' in the United Kingdom and elsewhere from the late 1930s was developed by opponents of the static theory he so derides.

The reason was simple. Static theory suppressed the information problem and thus could be interpreted as providing an intellectual foundation for a decentralised form of market socialism. Of all the intellectual achievements (and there is no doubting its brilliance) considered most dangerous to the free market in the 1950s and 1960s, Walrasian general equilibrium theory was at the top of the list. Instead of an 'auctioneer', a central 'planner' could attempt the same function—instructing decentralised factory managers to mimic the market by maximising profit whilst buying and selling at general equilibrium 'prices' calculated at the centre. Thus the 'planner' was as plausible as the 'auctioneer' in a world of full information, and market economists tried for decades to resist the elegant seductions of an approach which missed out the basic problem of economic life—imperfect information. Hutton informs us that the 'auctioneer' is a 'wild fantasy'[3] invented by market economists. The truth seems to be that, in the cycles of intellectual life, those on the defensive (whether believers in state intervention or the free market) accuse their opponents of naïve faith in the tenets of general equilibrium theory.

Free market theorists were thus prominent in the study of information problems. They wished to show that market processes were more effective at making use of dispersed information for social ends than processes based upon central planning.

This was the bone of contention in the famous 'calculation debate' between Lerner and Hayek in the 1940s, a debate that Hayek was for many years widely seen as having lost. It was also central to disputes about the nature of competition, with proponents of 'free markets' more inclined to emphasise its dynamic, disruptive, innovative side rather than the static, 'perfect' version propounded in the textbooks.

Reading Hutton[4] one might mistakenly assume that the approach of Keynes to time and uncertainty in chapter twelve of the *General Theory* is totally alien to market theorists. Judgements about the efficacy of state intervention in market processes might differ, but Keynes was articulating ideas that have strong affinities with the 'Austrian' tradition. Schumpeter[5] on the dynamics of capitalism, Hayek[6] on the use of dispersed knowledge, Shackle[7] on the role of expectation and profit, Wiseman[8] on the implications of uncertainty and subjectivism for control of the nationalised industries, Loasby[9] on the general problem of choice in the face of complexity, Kirzner[10] on the role of entrepreneurship—these were all students of market processes and the information problem. By what strange alchemy does Hutton transform the intellectual opponents of these writers into the high priesthood of 'free market' economics?

Institutions and Markets

Hutton defines the 'free market' agenda in a way which is extremely restrictive. Market exchange involves coming to agreements. For Hutton there is one quintessentially 'free market' type of contract—the spot-market contract. Economies cannot function efficiently if all contracts are of this variety. Labour services and many other complex goods and services cannot be traded as if they were foreign currencies, shares, minerals or agricultural commodities. Thus, Hutton argues, the 'free market' agenda is fatally flawed. Something more is required than spot markets and this something is a sophisticated set of institutions capable of encouraging the gains from trade (co-operative effort) even where problems of information and enforcement are severe.

By setting up the problem in this way, Hutton provides himself with an easy target and once more ignores a whole tradition of 'market orientated' analysis. Free market theory, as distinct from general equilibrium theory, is not devoid of institutional content. If the year were 1967 instead of 1997 one might have more sympathy with Hutton's irritation. For the last thirty years, however, economists have devoted a huge amount of attention to economic institutions. Indeed the literature is now so vast that it is sometimes referred to as 'The New Institutional Economics' in order to distinguish it from the 1930s variety of Veblen, Berle and Means.

Ronald Coase provided the key to this branch of economics.[11] In a celebrated sentence he remarked that 'there would seem to be a cost of using the price mechanism'. Since 1937, transaction cost analysis has been developed by many economists, most notably Armen Alchian,[12] Harold Demsetz,[13] and Oliver Williamson.[14] The essence of the transactions cost approach to institutions is that the contractual forms which we observe will depend upon the informational problems and the contractual hazards to which they are subject. Sometimes spot market arrangements will be efficient. Conditions in other circumstances might favour more durable, less closely specified, 'relational' contracts with 'the firm' setting up sophisticated 'governance structures' to protect a long-run association and to adjudicate in case of disputes.

In Coase's original analysis, institutional alternatives were confined to a simple bifurcation between 'firm' and 'market'. These two institutional forms were substitutes. Choice between them would be determined by the minimisation of transactions costs. The firm would have decisive advantages in respect of some types of transaction. Other transactions might equally clearly be better handled across outside markets. The boundary of the firm would be located where the advantages of firm and market were finely balanced and overall transactions costs were minimised.

Hutton mentions transactions costs[15] but asserts that 'free market strategy' is to 'open up any contract for competition and accept the lowest price'. Considered as a matter of the definition of terms, there is a sense in which this is correct. An institution contracting out a higher and higher proportion of its activities might be said to be following a 'free market strategy' as distinct from a strategy of 'internalisation'. But to infer from this that free market economic theorists regard such a strategy as always preferable, that market contracts always beat 'internal' arrangements, is a mistake. Free market thinkers, following Coasian logic, have argued for many years now that the likely outcome of market processes is a transactions cost minimising one. Further, and more normatively, they would argue that it is up to the people most intimately concerned with the relevant transactions to decide on the institutional context that can best cope with the hazards they expect to encounter.

The Evolution of Institutions

The nub of modern disputes is therefore much more subtle than Hutton is prepared to admit. The important question is whether relatively unfettered choice within a 'free market' can be expected to produce efficient institutional structures or whether active intervention by government or its agents is desirable. It is clear that Hutton believes in the necessity of state action, but his critique of 'market economics' is so off-target that it is largely irrelevant to establishing his case. In the absence of intervention, Hutton argues, institutions embodying durable commitments, high levels of trust, efficient levels of investment (especially in human capital) and co-operative effort will not develop. He is quite specific on this point: 'Nor can such relations be expected to appear from a Darwinian competitive struggle'.[16] As a matter of historical record, according to Hutton, 'the constitution of the Japanese firm and its relationship with government, finance and workforce is not a "natural" evolution'.[17] Most clearly of all: 'co-operative capitalism does not spontaneously emerge from free markets—it needs to be designed'.[18]

A curious aspect of Hutton's argument here is that he clearly recognises the evolutionary nature of economic competition although most of his fire power against the 'free market' position is earlier aimed at static general equilibrium theory. The fact that this static theory tells us nothing about institutions in no way allows us to deduce that an evolutionary and dynamic account might not provide greater insight. Indeed, Hutton cites with approval Robert Axelrod's book *The Evolution of Co-operation*. 'The strategy that works best' reports Hutton 'in hundreds of simulated games is to be straightforward rather than dishonest ... and above all to co-operate'.[19] The prospect of repeat dealing can result in a high pay-off to a strategy of 'tit for tat' and thus to a considerable level of purely self-interested co-operation. Apparently the 'selfish gene' does not preclude the evolution of co-operative behaviour either in social life or the natural world. Recent advances in game theory have thus confirmed the insight of political economists down the centuries that markets can be associated with large natural incentives to durable associations and honest dealing.

Hutton does not provide a succinct explanation of this apparent contradiction between the large social gains available through co-operation and the supposed inability of free agents to grasp them (though his whole book can be seen as an indirect exploration of this question). At some points he seems to offer a psychological explanation. In a truly free market there is 'constant temptation' not to commit or to 'cut and run' in pursuit of a better deal.[20] In Hirschman's terms,[21] it is too easy to 'exit' from an association rather than use 'voice' to pursue one's interests within it. Further, people discount the future at too high a rate for their own good—an argument of very long pedigree in the theory of public finance and welfare economics.

It seems reasonable to suppose that a successful institution will wish to avoid inefficient 'quits' and will therefore contrive to produce a level of 'dependency' on the part of its members. The sociologist Michael Hechter shows,[22] for example, how successful groups (by which he means those that have survived for a long time) ensure dependency on the part of their members. Hutton again notes many of the ways this dependency can be contrived in a commercial context. Wages above those available elsewhere (efficiency wages) and explicit or implicit 'bond-posting' devices or 'hostages' may give assurance of a durable commitment. But these devices can be chosen by contractors in pursuit of mutual advantage without government intervention. To say that 'free market theory has proved inadequate at explaining such apparently irrational behaviour' is once more to define free market theory as the theory of the spot-market contract. It is not at all clear why Hutton insists on presenting market processes as antithetical to institutions designed to elicit trust and durability of association. Institutional experiment is a part of the competitive market process.

The market undermines durable associations only in the sense that the utility derived from contracting at arm's length provides a benchmark or 'participation constraint' below which members of an institution cannot fall without putting the survival of the institution in jeopardy. Exit is indeed always an option, but if there are gains from co-operation in a team and these gains or 'rents' (payments in excess of the alternatives available outside the team) are suitably distributed, defection will not occur. Hutton has to explain why firms are unable to adjust their corporate structures and constitutions to the circumstances which face them and so to produce the level of dependency that they require in their suppliers, workers or financiers. It is not as if institutions are all structured alike. Partnerships, co-operatives, profit-sharing firms, non-profit enterprises, labour-managed firms, closely owned private companies as well as public joint stock corporations can all be observed in the United Kingdom. There may, as Hutton rightly emphasises, be many different varieties of capitalism, but he downplays the extent to which all of them can be observed competing within the confines of a single economy.

Hutton will reply that his criticism of British capitalism is 'systemic'. Granted the existence of a few exceptional examples of firms emulating Japanese norms with their suppliers or workers, economic forces in the United Kingdom warp the institutional structures which survive in the direction of the short-term rather than long-term end of the contractual spectrum. The villain of the piece is a financial system consisting of 'commercial' rather than 'industrial' banks and a stock market dominated by institutional investors. The desire for liquidity is so strong that it inhibits the provision of long term 'committed' finance and makes it impossible for firms to develop the trust of their suppliers, the loyalty and skills of their employees, the innovation which will improve products and processes, or the capital stock necessary to raise productivity and compete effectively in overseas markets. The Anglo-American stock market-based system of finance is therefore at the centre of Hutton's criticism of British institutions.

The important theoretical proposition here is that individual agents are somehow trapped by the system. Evolutionary processes may result in a system that is inefficient and yet beyond the power of any individual firm or group of firms to change. This possibility is illustrated by the crossroads game.[23]

Rules of the road are to a degree self enforcing. It is in everyone's individual interest to know what the rules are in order to predict the behaviour of others and to achieve an orderly coordination of road traffic. As a mental experiment, how might we envisage such rules evolving spontaneously? Where two roads cross, motorists may give way or maintain speed. The payoff to these strategies will depend upon the behaviour of other motorists. Over time (on repeated plays) conventions may emerge. For example, the convention that motorists on the relatively minor road should give way to motorists on the major road might become established. As the proportion of motorists adopting this convention rises above a critical level, there will be a clear private incentive for the remaining motorists to comply. In principle, however, it is conceivable that the converse convention might emerge. Motorists on the major road might defer to those on the minor one. This convention would be equally self-enforcing and difficult to change once it had become established. We might expect that the delays and slower speeds to the larger number of vehicles on the major road might make the second convention less socially efficient than the first. Yet it would take the simultaneous collective agreement of all motorists or the intervention of the state to change the rules.

Although Hutton does not develop this particular strand of reasoning or cite the relevant literature, it is clear that he views the financial system, corporate governance and transactional relations in the United Kingdom as somewhat analogous to the crossroads game. Institutions have evolved over time which he believes are socially inefficient but which effectively trap individuals and firms. We cannot always rely on the processes of competitive evolution to produce efficient institutions.

A major problem with this theory, however, is to show that transactions costs are so high, and systemic effects so widespread, that groups of financial institutions and firms could not experiment with alternative governance arrangements if the potential gains were significant enough. In the crossroads game it is obvious why this cannot occur. The game involves no direct communication between the players. Even in arm's-length Britain, however, bankers, investment fund managers and corporate directors are capable of talking with each other. Marginal rather than systemic change in pursuit of competitive advantage may be possible, in which case Hutton's appeal for root and branch reform is unnecessary and misconceived. The usual processes of entrepreneurship and competition will suffice to move the system in the direction of greater social efficiency.

A further problem is that the alleged superiority of German and Japanese models of corporate governance is open to doubt. Years of relatively high rates of growth of Gross National Product, investment, labour productivity and a commanding trade performance have led to uncritical acceptance of the superiority of Japanese institutions. Most people are instinctive mercantilists and admire state-sponsored export success. Both in Germany and Japan, however, recent years have seen much more faltering progress and the beginnings of a re-appraisal of the strengths and weaknesses of their systems.

Corporate Governance: An Alternative View

(i) **Japanese Institutions Re-Examined**

If the perceived relative failure of the United Kingdom economy since 1945 has resulted in a loss of confidence in its institutions, more recent world events have contributed to a similar re-appraisal of the institutions of other countries. It is a curious aspect of the modern debate about corporate governance that while the major critics of the market-orientated system are American and British, some of the most outspoken critics of the bank-orientated system are Japanese. Mochizuki dismisses the view that the Japanese corporation pursues desirable long-term strategies in investment and research and development (R and D) as a myth.[24] 'This tendency also could be construed as a lack of accountability due to insufficient corporate governance, rather than far-sighted management'. Long term investment 'caused major disasters to many Japanese corporations after the bubble burst of the Japanese economy in the early 1990s'.[25] He sees corporate boards as full of 'insiders' unwilling to grasp the necessity of changing course and able to squander shareholders' funds. 'Stable employment and corporate loyalty praised by many western commentators could generate stagnation and xenophobia.'

From a Japanese point of view, the institutions that served in the post-war world to close the gap between US and Japanese income levels could represent a hindrance to further advance. Akio Mikuni argues that Japan must 'shake off its anachronistic wartime footing and set the stage for a new era of market-led economic growth'.[26] It is thus possible to see Japanese institutions as a hangover from an era in which economic objectives were relatively simple, and in which the encouragement of discipline, conformity, loyalty and consensus were capable of generating high returns. In the new (post catch-up) era the ability to develop and adapt to new technologies, to encourage mobility between sectors and to make difficult investment decisions in high-risk areas may require adjustments to Japanese institutional structures—adjustments in the direction of market norms.

For several years now, writers on business have been drawing attention to gradual changes in Japanese economic organisation. Companies have responded to the information boom and the increasing technical links between hitherto separate industries by a policy of diversification. Ubukata[27] notes that this has required the movement of workers between companies, 'the breakdown of the lifetime employment system' and the undermining of the seniority system.[28] *The Economist*[29] noted that 'Nissan ..poaches experienced employees from other firms for many of the new businesses, such as mobile telecommunications, into which it is diversifying'. Mochizuki argues that 'lifetime employment is a phenomenon only temporary for the period after 1945 and limited to larger corporations' and that it will never again be the same 'as at the time of the continuous economic growth'.[30] The academic literature has also charted these changes. Clark and Ogawa show that by the mid-1980s in Japan the value of a year of job tenure in a particular firm had fallen below the value of a year's general experience.[31] The incentive to remain with a single firm was falling. The events of the early 1990s can only have reinforced this trend.

In the financial sector too, changed conditions are influencing Japanese corporate governance. A regulated system designed to produce low-cost finance for large-scale industry has been liberalised and some studies have concluded that the cost of capital is no longer lower in Japan compared with the United States. Further, the absence of capital gains (indeed substantial capital losses) on share holdings in recent years has put many banks and other financial institutions under pressure. As that pressure has mounted the patience of these long-term investors has been sorely tried and its limits tested. In this process attention is being diverted to some familiar areas. Stefan Wagstyl, for example, records the falling capital spending in Japanese companies even in areas such as research and development.[32] With Japanese firms unable to escape the emerging constraints on growth, he argues that 'the chase after sales seems certain to give way to a pursuit of profits'.

Disenchantment with bank-orientated systems of corporate governance derives therefore from the very features which make it attractive to critics of the market-orientated system. For the latter, long term stable relationships give rise to well-informed owners willing to sacrifice immediate returns for the future development of the firm. The alternative view is that long-term stable relationships between financial institutions and firms ultimately lead to a system which is too forgiving, permits empire building on the part of managers, makes radical innovation very difficult, and risks the squandering of resources on unproductive investment.

(ii) **Empirical Evidence on Short-termism**

Defenders of the Anglo-American system argue that a great deal of evidence exists which contradicts the short-termist critique. If, for example, investment in R and D is discouraged by the stock market it is odd that studies have found that announcements of R and D expenditure and long-term capital expenditure more generally are associated with stock price increases.[33] If firms who invested in research attracted takeover raiders who tried to steal the returns to these 'undervalued' assets why could not Hall[34] detect any effect of mergers on R and D performance?

Studies of takeovers during the 1980s showed that share prices of target companies rose sharply at the announcement of a bid.[35] Critics believe that this premium represented the present value of a redistribution of income towards shareholders of target companies rather than gains in productive efficiency. Jensen argues,[36] however, that social gains amounting to about eight per cent of the combined value of the companies involved were achieved by the average takeover in the United States. The takeover mechanism, in Jensen's view, was particularly effective in the 1980s in prizing resources away from cash-rich companies in the oil and other industries. These resources would otherwise have been wasted by managers on low-return projects within the target firms rather than used for higher-yielding projects elsewhere.[37] The use of surpluses in the petroleum industry for further exploration, for example, made it cheaper at one stage to acquire reserves by buying companies than by actual search. In the process of takeover, cash was disgorged to the shareholders of target companies who were then free to consider alternative uses for their funds. Other studies confirm the effectiveness of the takeover as a constraint on managerial moral hazard. In the United States, some individual states restrict takeover activity in the banking sector while others do not. Schranz finds that banking firms are more profitable in those states which have an active takeover market.[38]

For defenders of the market-orientated system of corporate governance, therefore, it is as reasonable to accuse the bank-orientated system of over-long-termism as it is to accuse the market system of short-termism. The Anglo-American system offers the advantages of great flexibility, an effective weapon against managerial waste, and a means of preventing over-investment whether this be in oil reserves, physical equipment or the currently fashionable areas of training and research.

Corporate Governance and the Constitution

Hutton's book is so wide-ranging in its critique of British institutions that even a sceptical reader is likely to find much to agree with. His scathing attack on the power and patronage of an over-mighty executive and the centralising tendency of the state is in the best traditions of British liberalism. Much of this reinforces the indictment of centralising government policy pursued by successive Conservative administrations set out by Simon Jenkins.[39] The connection between these constitutional issues and the supposed inefficiency of British economic institutions, however, is not properly established.

That broad constitutional issues are important in the long run in encouraging or inhibiting economic development is not disputed. Freedom from arbitrary executive power, security of property, the development of the common law—these products of the English revolution of the 17th century had far reaching effects. As Douglas North puts it:

> the fundamental changes in the English polity as a consequence of the Glorious Revolution were a critical contributing factor to the development of the English economy.[40]

The links between Britain's existing constitutional arrangements and the supposed dominance of an inefficient form of capitalism are much less clear. Hutton proceeds more by loose analogy than by logical inference—'Running a company is a reflection of running the nation'(p. 11)—and believes that greater decentralisation of political power would be associated with more decentralised financial institutions and with changed attitudes to the governance of economic institutions. Some direct effects on particular institutions at present governed as quangos answering to central government might be expected and welcome. A substantial impact on the governance of commercial and industrial firms is a different matter entirely. A measure of constitutional reform may be supported even by those who believe that the Anglo-American financial system is one of the elements in the British economy that is working well.

Conclusion

Capitalism's 'golden rule' was once defined by Robertson and Dennison as 'where the risk lies, there lies the control also'.[41] A more modern rendering would probably run 'where the firm dependency lies, there lies the control'.[42] Hutton's appeal for stakeholder capitalism does not contradict this principle. Stakeholders can be seen as team-dependent resources. In the simple world of classical capitalism, shareholders could be regarded as the dependent group because others could escape into the outside market and costlessly 'desert the sinking ship'. Modern thinking would emphasise the existence of dependent labour with specific skills as well as dependent suppliers with accumulated 'know-how' and experience. The value of these resources in alternative employments is less than their value inside the firm. There is no doubt that this dependency raises important 'governance' issues. The main dispute, however, is not whether durable associations and the development of specific skills are important, but whether institutional evolution in a 'free market' context is capable of handling them.

One of the ironies of Hutton's approach is his insistence that successful forms of capitalism require 'conscious design' (p. 10).

The centralist power of the British state will presumably be required to achieve his recommended design change. If so, a period of intervention in institutional structure as great as that experienced under the last four Conservative governments would be necessary. Instead of the Tories' obsession with arm's-length contract would come an obsession with stakeholder rights, consultation procedures, board structures, takeover rules and so forth. Obligational contractual relations would replace arm's-length 'contracting out' as the British government's latest big idea. The case for such a systemic change, however, is much weaker than Hutton believes. A government determined to permit institutional experiment and to allow differing governance arrangements to compete with each other would be more likely to produce long-run success and would represent a truly 'free market' approach to institutions.

Stakeholder Theory:
The Defective State It's In

Elaine Sternberg

Stakeholding has been widely offered, by Will Hutton and many others, as a corrective to perceived defects of society and business, and as an alternative model of corporate governance. Indeed, it is now advocated so commonly as to have become a new orthodoxy. Far from being a source of improvements, however, stakeholder theory is fundamentally misguided, incapable of providing better governance, economic performance or business conduct. The stakeholder doctrine is indeed intrinsically incompatible with all substantive organisational objectives, and undermines both private property and accountability.

The Meaning of Stakeholding

As Dr. Johnson might well have said, there is much in the notion of stakeholding that is sound and original ... unfortunately, that which is sound is not original, and that which is original is not sound. To the extent that 'stakeholding' serves as more than a general panegyric, it tends to be used in one of three main ways. Two are largely anodyne. If taking a stakeholder approach simply means recognising that, on the whole, people are more likely to take an interest in a process when they are materially concerned in its outcome, then 'stakeholding' is neither distinctive nor new. Similarly, if stakeholding simply means recognising that a variety

Versions of this paper have been published as 'Stakeholder Theory Exposed' in *The Corporate Governance Quarterly*, HK, Vol. 2, No. 1, March 1996, pp.4-18; in *Economic Affairs*, Vol. 16, No. 3, Summer 1996, pp.36-38; and as 'The Defects of Stakeholder Theory' in *Corporate Governance: An International Review*, Blackwells, Vol. 5, No. 1, January 1997, pp.3-10.

of interests must ordinarily be taken into account when pursuing organisational objectives, then all that is exceptional about stakeholding is the label.

It is when force is added to those two notions that stakeholding becomes something distinctive: the doctrine that organisations should be run for the benefit of, and should be accountable to, all their stakeholders. It is in this sense that stakeholding is advocated by Will Hutton. In 'The Stakeholder Society', Hutton proposes stakeholding as the model for a 'wholesale restructuring' (p. 8)[1] of Britain's financial, welfare and political systems, through a reform programme backed by 'regulation and intervention' (p. 10). Unfortunately, like most of the other notions presented in 'The Stakeholder Society', this conception of stakeholding is wholly misguided.[2]

In 'The Stakeholder Society', Hutton never actually defines what he means by 'stakeholder'. Instead, he calls upon the term's established use in management literature (p. 9). What 'stakeholder' means there, however, has changed radically since the term was first introduced in 1963.[3] Stakeholders were originally identified as those without whom a business corporation could not survive, those in whom the business had a stake. Now, in contrast, stakeholders are more commonly identified as those who have a stake *in* a business. According to R. Edward Freeman, a prominent stakeholder theorist:

> A stakeholder in an organization is (by definition) any group or individual who can affect or is affected by the achievement of the organization's objectives.[4]

When 'stakeholder' is understood in this way, the number of groups identified as stakeholders is unlimited. Whereas stakeholders were originally those groups necessary for a business's survival, the popular modern characterisation excludes all criteria of materiality, immediacy and legitimacy: a stakeholder is simply any group or individual who affects or is in any way affected by an organisation. Terrorists and competitors,[5] vegetation,[6] nameless sea creatures[7] and generations yet unborn[8] are amongst the many groups which are now seriously considered to be business stakeholders. Indeed, given the increasing internationalisation of modern life, and the global connections made possible by improved transportation, telecommunications and computing power, those affected (at least distantly and indirectly) by any given organisation, and thus counting as its stakeholders, include virtually everyone, everything, everywhere.

A concept this broad would seem to be necessary if stakeholding is to underpin a radical reform of all society. Throughout this discussion, therefore, 'stakeholder' will be used in this inclusive sense, to refer to all those who can affect, or are affected by, an organisation.[9] The 'stakeholder doctrine' ('stakeholder theory') that will be analysed is the view that organisations should be run for the benefit of all their stakeholders. It is an essential tenet of this doctrine that organisations are accountable to all their stakeholders, and that the proper objective of management is to balance stakeholders' competing interests.

Stakeholder Theory is Incompatible with Substantive Objectives

The first thing to be said against the stakeholder doctrine is that, whatever else it may be, it is not a sensible model of, or even compatible with, either business or most provision of social welfare—though these are precisely the institutions that Hutton is most eager to reform. The stakeholder doctrine requires organisations to be run for the benefit of all their stakeholders; it therefore precludes all objectives which favour particular stakeholders. Business understood as the activity of maximising long-term owner value[10] is automatically ruled out. Hutton and most stakeholder advocates would probably be quite pleased. But stakeholder theory also excludes the quite different aims of maximising value-added for customers and improving benefits for employees. Even worse for Hutton, stakeholder theory precludes organisations from having as their goals educating the young or housing the homeless or curing the sick. Since all organisations with substantive ends aim at something other than 'balanced stakeholder benefits', they are all ruled out by the stakeholder doctrine. According to stakeholder theory, there is only one type of legitimate organisation, the one that balances stakeholder benefits.

But 'balancing stakeholder benefits' is itself an unworkable objective. First, since stakeholders are all those who can affect or are affected by the organisation, the number of people whose benefits need to be taken into account is infinite. For a balance to be struck, their numbers must somehow be limited. But stakeholder theory offers no guidance as to how the appropriate individuals or groups should be selected. Even the ostensibly simple category 'employee' leaves many questions open. Are temporary employees to be included in the category, or just permanent staff? Are part-timers to be included on the same basis as full-timers? Does the category of 'employee' include pensioners? Former employees? Probationary trainees? Potential recruits? Some non-arbitrary criterion needs to be found if these questions are to be answered satisfactorily. But stakeholder theory offers none. Furthermore, individuals are often members of more than one stakeholder group. Employees may be shareholders; shareholders may be customers; suppliers may be creditors. In which capacity or capacities are they to be included in the calculation?

Second, even if the stakeholder groups could be identified and restricted to a manageable number, stakeholder theory does not explain what should count as a benefit for the purposes of balancing benefits. Is everything that a stakeholder regards as beneficial to be included in the calculation? And how are the managers to know what stakeholders consider to be benefits? Despite the simplifying and often presumptuous assumptions which are commonly made, even members of the same notional stakeholder constituency often have significantly different views as to what is beneficial. Some employees want higher wages, others want shorter hours; some regard more responsibility as a benefit, others consider it to be a burden. How are stakeholders' divergent perceptions of benefit to be discerned and entered into the balance?

Third, and most fundamentally, even if the relevant benefits could somehow be identified, stakeholder theory provides no guidance as to how the balance is to be struck. Given the divergent interests of the different stakeholder groups, that which benefits one group will often harm another. Even within a notional stakeholder group, benefits may well conflict with each other. Higher wages for some employees may require layoffs of others, and money spent on redundancy payments or on pensions is not available for wages. Stakeholder theory does not indicate which of these benefits is to be preferred, nor how conflicting interests are to be balanced. Are stakeholder interests all strictly equal? Are some more important than others? If so, which are they? And when, and by how much, and why?

Stakeholder theory gives no clue as to how to rank or reconcile the normally conflicting interests of stakeholders.

It may now be protested that such problems are, nonetheless, routinely resolved in practice. And indeed they are. But the way that they are resolved is by using the substantive goal of the organisation as a decision criterion. If the purpose of the operation is to maximise long-term owner value, or to produce the environmentally-friendliest widgits, or to provide employment for the blind, that purpose enables managers to identify which groups need to be considered, and which of their perceived benefits are relevant and legitimate; it indicates how benefits are to be ranked, and how conflicts are to be resolved. The only way that the stakeholder doctrine can be made workable is to employ the very substantive objectives that it explicitly rejects.[11] Like a parasite, the stakeholder doctrine is viable only so long as its targets withstand its attacks.

Stakeholder Theory is Incompatible with Corporate Governance

So the stakeholder doctrine cannot serve either to illuminate or to improve business or the provision of social welfare. Nor can it provide a workable model for any organisation with substantive objectives. Perhaps then, despite its origins, the stakeholder doctrine should be considered instead as a model of corporate governance. Hutton certainly intends it to be the basis of 'corporate governance reformed to reflect the various interests that converge on the firm' (p. 9). But unfortunately, stakeholding is not capable of that either. Stakeholder theory is as incompatible with the conditions and operations of corporate governance as it is with the objective of business or specific forms of social welfare.

To see why that is so, it is useful to review what is actually meant by 'corporate governance'. Because the corporate form makes it easy for ownership to be detached from management, mechanisms are needed for ensuring that corporate actions, assets and agents are devoted to achieving the corporate purpose established by the shareholders.[12] Whether that purpose is business or charity or education, the aim of corporate governance is to make sure that it is the shareholders' stipulated objective that governs the corporation and all its actions and agents.[13]

The key concept in corporate governance is accountability: the accountability of directors to shareholders, and the accountability of corporate employees and other corporate agents to the corporation via the directors. Stakeholder theory is inimical to them both. And this is not surprising. The stakeholder doctrine does, after all, explicitly deny that corporations should be accountable to their owners: it is an essential principle of the stakeholder doctrine that corporations should be equally accountable to *all* their stakeholders. This core doctrine is, however, not only wholly unjustified, but unworkable. An organisation that is accountable to everyone, is actually accountable to no one: accountability that is diffuse is effectively non-existent. Multiple accountability can only function if everyone involved accepts a clear common purpose. But that is what the stakeholder doctrine conspicuously rejects.

Furthermore, the stakeholder doctrine provides no effective standard against which corporate agents can be judged. 'Balancing stakeholder interests' is an ill-defined notion, which cannot serve as an objective performance measure; managers responsible for interpreting as well as implementing it are effectively left free to pursue their own arbitrary ends. Accordingly, the stakeholder doctrine gives full rein to arrogant and unresponsive managements, and to extravagance in respect of salaries, premises and perks. The stakeholder doctrine licenses resistance to takeover bids that would benefit shareholders, and permits the pursuit of empire-building acquisitions that make little business sense. The stakeholder doctrine indulges exploitation by lenders, and inferior performance by employees and suppliers. So despite the pious hopes which are so often attached to the stakeholder doctrine, it is unlikely to improve either corporate performance or corporate governance.

But the prognosis is even worse. The stakeholder doctrine is not only prone to impair corporate governance: it is *bound* to do so. Most conditions of employment include an at least nominal commitment to furthering the employer's purposes. Stakeholder theory, in contrast, requires managers to ignore those purposes, and balance stakeholder interests instead. Inciting betrayal of trust is a particularly ironic feature in a theory supposed to promote better conduct.

The Stakeholder Doctrine of Accountability is Unjustified

So the stakeholder doctrine cannot serve as a useful model of corporate governance in any traditional sense; it destroys, rather than supports, conventional corporate accountability. Can the stakeholder doctrine justify its alternative doctrine, that corporations, and more generally organisations, should be accountable to all their stakeholders?

The first thing to note is that, although this precept is both essential to the stakeholder doctrine and highly contentious, attempts are seldom made to justify it. Hutton certainly does not try to. He simply points to features of the German and Japanese systems that he finds particularly congenial, and recommends that British institutions be remodelled to include them (p. 4).[14]

Most stakeholder theorists proceed without argument from the undeniable fact that organisations are affected by and affect certain factors, to the unjustified conclusion that organisations should be accountable to them. But that cannot be right. Organisations are affected by gravity and affect employment levels, but they are not, and logically could not be, held to account by them. Natural forces and economic statistics are not the sorts of things that can hold agents to account. Equally, organisations affect and are affected by burglars and terrorists and competitors, but could not sensibly be accountable to them. That an organisation must take many factors into account, does not give them any right to hold it to account. Nor does the fact that various groups are affected by an organisation give them any right to control it. If stakeholder theorists are to maintain their claim that organisations are accountable to all their stakeholders, some convincing argument is needed.

The Performance Argument

One (typically implicit) argument for accountability to all stakeholders is that which points to performance. It is sometimes suggested that the best way to achieve business success is not to concentrate narrowly on financial outcomes, but to strive instead to delight customers, to empower employees, to form lasting partnerships with suppliers, etc. And to the extent that such strategies enhance motivation, or improve quality, they may well be justified as effective means for achieving the business end. But the practical success of stakeholder-oriented strategies does not and cannot justify accountability to stakeholders. Establishing accountability to all stakeholders requires showing that they have legitimate authority, not that they are functionally useful. As the property of its owners, a business is properly accountable only to them.[15]

Treating Stakeholders as Ends

A related argument alleges that organisations should be accountable to all their stakeholders because otherwise those stakeholders would be treated merely as means to others' ends. This is a strategy much favoured by one of Hutton's acknowledged 'intellectual influences' (p. 13), John Kay.[16] Treating stakeholders as ends is deemed to be wrong for two quite distinct reasons. First, it is thought to be a less effective way of achieving substantive objectives. This may sometimes be true, but as shown above, it is irrelevant to justifying accountability.

More fundamentally, it is sometimes claimed that treating stakeholders as means to others' ends is morally wrong. Although commonly associated with Kantian philosophy,[17] that assertion is, nevertheless, quite unjustified. To the extent that stakeholders include environmental features and abstract groupings, the dictum makes no sense: even for Kant it is only persons—rational moral agents—who must be treated as ends in themselves. Moreover, treating persons as ends in themselves merely means respecting their moral agency. That neither precludes persons' being instrumental in serving others' ends, nor requires accountability to them.

Far from supporting the stakeholder doctrine, the notion of treating persons as ends actually provides a strong argument against it. Respecting persons as moral agents requires allowing persons to choose their own ends. But this is what the stakeholder doctrine conspicuously fails to do. Instead of respecting the ends freely chosen by consenting moral agents, stakeholder theory systematically and forcibly overrides them, in favour of balancing stakeholder benefits. 'Treating persons as ends' is not even compatible with stakeholder theory; it certainly cannot justify the stakeholder doctrine of accountability to all stakeholders.

The Parallel with Government[18]

Another unsuccessful argument for accountability to all stakeholders comes from confusing corporate governance with government. Democratic governments, it is alleged, are accountable to their citizens; citizens are equal under the law, and are entitled to representation and a vote. Regarding stakeholders in an organisation as citizens of that organisation, some commentators have assumed that stakeholders have comparable rights.

This conclusion is unfounded for several reasons. First, the argument overlooks the special nature of government: government is different from all other organisations because of its monopoly on the legitimate use of physical violence.[19] It is because government has the power forcibly to deprive the governed of their lives,[20] liberty and property, that it is vital for those subject to its power to have a say in how that power is used.

Comparable accountability is neither required nor justified in non-governmental organisations. Unlike government, ordinary organisations cannot legally use force to compel anyone to do anything; they cannot even enforce their own contracts without recourse to the courts. Since organisations have no coercive power, there is no need to hold them accountable for its use. Those who do not wish to comply with an organisation's decision or policy can simply leave;[21] in ordinary organisations, unlike in government, participants can ordinarily vote with their feet. The parallel with government thus fails at the outset: non-governmental organisations are too different from governments for the comparison to be valid.

Even if the parallel could be sustained, however, the stakeholder theorists' conclusion still would not follow. Contrary to the argument's assumption, even democratic governments are not accountable to all their citizens. Those who have been certified insane or who are underage or are convicted felons typically may not vote. Until quite recently youths aged 18 to 21 lacked the franchise. And in Britain, peers of the realm still may not vote in elections for the House of Commons, even though they are undoubtedly affected by its actions. Still less are governments accountable to all their stakeholders. Foreigners affect and are affected by governmental actions but have no say in controlling them; foreign visitors, even long-term foreign residents, suffer taxation without representation. Corporations are clearly affected by and affect government, but cannot vote, even though they are domestic legal persons.

The parallel with government therefore provides no support for the conclusion that organisations should be accountable to all their stakeholders. Even as democratic governments are accountable only to some of their citizens—to sane, non-felonious adults—organisations are properly accountable only to some of their stakeholders—for corporations, to the shareholders and those with whom the corporation has entered into specific contractual agreements. So the parallel with government cannot sustain the stakeholder theorists' claim.

The Social Contract Argument

Another defence that stakeholder theorists sometimes offer for their position is a form of 'social contract' argument. According to this line of reasoning, organisations are accountable to all their stakeholders because organisations use society's resources and enjoy special privileges from society. In exchange for society's consenting to provide the resources and privileges that they need to exist, organisations become accountable to society. Though superficially plausible, this argument is based on confusions about the nature of both consent and of accountability; it, too, does not support the stakeholder theorists' conclusion.

Consent normally means one of two things: (tacit) agreement or formal authorisation. In the sense of tacit agreement, it is certainly true that organisations require the consent of society. Consider a business. Unless members of society acting as investors agree to provide capital, unless members of society acting as employees agree to provide labour, unless members of society acting as suppliers agree to provide materials, etc., businesses cannot operate. And unless members of society acting as customers agree to buy their products and services, businesses cannot survive.

But though organisations certainly depend on the tacit agreement—indeed the willing cooperation—of the members of society, that does not give society at large any right to hold them to account. Being affected by a group, even needing to be functionally responsive to a group, is quite different from being accountable to that group. Organisations must indeed take various groups into account. But they are answerable to those groups only insofar as the law or specific contractual arrangements have made them so.[22] Members of society can withdraw their cooperation, but they have no general authority to hold organisations to account.

Perhaps, then, the 'social contract' argument for accountability to all stakeholders relies on the notion of consent as formal permission. On the face of it, this is less plausible. It is a defining characteristic of free societies that whatever is not expressly prohibited is allowed, and that strict limits apply as to what may be officially prohibited. Since individuals already possess all the powers they need to run organisations, consent in the sense of formal permission is seldom necessary.

There are some cases, of course, in which formal permissions are required to establish or operate organisations, especially when organisations enjoy special privileges. To constitute an English corporation, for example, and enjoy separate legal existence and limited liability for shareholders, it is necessary to file a Memorandum and Articles of Association with the Registrar of Companies, and comply with the requirements of the Companies Acts.

When such formal permissions are needed, however, the privileges conceded and the considerations expected are both explicitly stipulated. So are the procedures for obtaining them: typically, designated undertakings must be submitted to designated authorities, often accompanied by the payment of designated fees. To compensate for their special privileges, for example, British corporations must pay UK corporation taxes. Contrary to the stakeholder theorists' claim, the obligations involved are specific, and specific to the kind of organisation: even organisations which require formal authorisation have no general obligation to society to which they can be held accountable by all stakeholders. The claim to such accountability is no more justified by formal permission than it is by tacit agreement.

On what, then, is the stakeholder theorists' argument based? The core of their argument is actually very simple: organisations are liable to control by society because they need society's permission to operate. Since organisations already exist, and do so routinely, however, this statement looks rather like a threat: organisations must submit themselves to society's requirements, because otherwise society will retract its consent. If this refers to the fact that the members of society may withdraw the willing cooperation that organisations need to function, all well and good. But as already shown, that possibility does not make organisations accountable to their stakeholders. If, instead, this argument refers to some more active way in which society might turn against organisations, then the stakeholder theorists seem to be relying on what looks very like extortion: agreeing not to inflict harm in exchange for appeasement is not entering into a social contract, but running a protection racket.

The undeniable fact that some groups may have power over an organisation—even the power to destroy that organisation—does not, and cannot, give those groups legitimate authority over the organisation, or the right to hold it to account. The fact that muggers may kill you if you do not surrender your money, does not give muggers the right to your money or to your life; it simply means that they are capable of theft and murder. Claims to justify accountability require demonstrations of entitlement, not displays of raw power.

Stakeholder Theory Undermines Private Property, Agency and Wealth

So the stakeholder theorists have not been able to justify their claim that organisations should be accountable to all their stakeholders. Since the stakeholder doctrine is so widely accepted even without justification, however, it is important to recognise just how serious its implications are. In particular, it is essential to understand that the stakeholder doctrine undermines two of the most fundamental features that characterise modern society: private property and the duties that agents owe to principals.

Hutton is quite explicit that his version of the stakeholder society would involve prescriptions that 'are very different from those of free-market theory' (p. 8). It

> ...would involve wholesale restructuring [of the financial system]... to establish patterns of more committed ownership and more long-term lending... financial obstacles to takeovers... and corporate governance reformed to reflect the various interests that converge on the firm... This is the central idea of the stakeholder economy.... such a reform programme [requires]... regulation and intervention (pp. 8-9).

Hutton is less explicit about the extent to which his proposals would involve a wholesale denial of property rights. But the stakeholder doctrine necessarily undermines private property, because it denies owners the right to determine how their property will be used. Insofar as assets are held or utilised by organisations, the stakeholder doctrine stipulates that those assets should be used for the benefit of all stakeholders. The owners of those assets are thereby prevented from devoting their property unequivocally to the ends of their choice, whether those ends are maximising owner value, housing the homeless or finding a cure for cancer. It may be argued that since the stakeholder doctrine concerns only organisational property, this is a small infringement. But since most property is manufactured, financed, distributed or otherwise processed through organisations, it would leave almost no property subject to owner control.

Stakeholder theorists sometimes attempt to justify curtailing property rights by indicating that property rights are seldom absolute. But the fact that some limitations may apply is not an argument for allowing others: the abolition of slavery does not justify the confiscation of land. As importantly, the fact that property rights may be weakly enforced, provides no justification for violating them. An overworked or lazy police force may make theft easier to accomplish; it does not give robbers the right to one's goods. Despite what stakeholder theorists suggest, the fact that shareholders are sometimes unwilling or unable actively to protect their interests does not entitle other stakeholders to commandeer corporate property.[23]

The stakeholder doctrine does not just attack property rights; it also denies the duty that agents owe to principals. Whenever one entrusts one's assets or affairs to another, the agent/principal relationship is invoked. It arises in respect of corporate directors and corporate managers; it also exists in every case of employment, whatever the form of the establishment. Agents' duty to principals is also central to the conduct of civil servants and armies, lawyers and investment managers, school teachers and motor mechanics. The stakeholder doctrine makes this critical relationship unworkable by denying that agents have any particular duty to their principals. According to the stakeholder doctrine, organisational agents are equally accountable to all stakeholders—and thus to no one.

Given the pervasive importance of agent/principal relationships, and the central role of private property in enabling economic activity and political liberty, neither should be surrendered without very good cause. The stakeholder doctrine should therefore be steadfastly resisted in all its manifestations. Corporate mission statements and political rhetoric promoting the stakeholder doctrine may seem innocuous, but they are expressions of a doctrine that is both deeply dangerous and wholly unjustified.

Why, then, is the stakeholder doctrine so popular? One reason is that its implications are seldom recognised. Another is that the stakeholder doctrine seems to offer a free lunch; it attracts those who would like to enjoy the benefits of business without the discipline of business. It particularly appeals to the those with much to gain from undermining accountability, including politicians and the business managers who would like to have the power and prestige and perks of office without the concomitant responsibility. The stakeholder doctrine also appeals to the promoters of worthy 'causes', who believe they would be the beneficiaries if business profits were diverted from business owners.

But they are mistaken: nothing comes from nothing. The wealth that they want from business will not be available if the essential business objective of maximising long-term owner value is forsaken, and investors are not allowed to reap the benefits of their investments. In the spurious expectation of achieving vaguely 'nicer' behaviour, the stakeholder approach would sacrifice not only property rights and accountability, but also the wealth-creating capabilities of business strictly understood.

Conclusion: The Appropriate Use of the Stakeholder Concept

So the stakeholder doctrine is both misguided and mistaken. But this does not mean that there is no legitimate use for the concept of stakeholder. There are indeed two distinct ways in which the concept can be detached from the pernicious stakeholder doctrine and be valuably employed.

As a Convenient Label

First, it is useful as a label. Even—indeed especially—in its broad interpretation, 'stakeholder' serves as a convenient collective noun for the groups and individuals that organisations have always needed to take into account when pursuing their substantive objectives. Stakeholders need to be considered both to improve organisations' chances of achieving their objectives, and to ensure that their conduct is ethical.

Consider business. Although its responsibilities to stakeholders are limited to those created by law and specific agreements, business cannot afford to ignore any stakeholder concern that might affect its ability to generate long-term owner value. In order to operate, business must secure the willing cooperation of diverse groups of people. It must therefore consider the preferences not just of owners, but of employees and customers, of suppliers and lenders, of regulators and environmental activists. Equally, to be ethical, a business must treat all its stakeholders ethically. Ethical treatment does not, however, mean equating all stakeholders' interests with those of the owners; it simply means treating all stakeholders with 'distributive justice' and 'ordinary decency'.[24]

As the Key to 'Social Responsibility'

In addition to being a useful label for all those individuals and groups which have to be taken into account, 'stakeholder' can also help to illuminate the proper meaning of 'social responsibility'.

Consider business again. Although only owners have the right to change the business's objectives,

> ... everyone can influence business conduct. By choosing whether or not, and to what extent, to support particular businesses with their investment or custom or labour, everyone can contribute to the economic conditions that critically affect business decisions. If, therefore, individuals have views as to how business should be conducted, they should ensure that their individual choices accurately reflect those views... When each potential stakeholder—otherwise known as every member of society—acts conscientiously in his personal capacity, and strategically bestows or withholds his economic support on the basis of his moral values, then the operation of market forces will automatically lead businesses to reflect those values.[25]

It is as such 'conscientious stakeholding' that social responsibility is properly understood.[26] To the extent that the term 'stakeholder' helps remind people of their individual responsibilities to act conscientiously, it can serve a second valuable function.

In summary, then, stakeholder notions as they are commonly used are either anodyne or fundamentally flawed. If they simply highlight the importance of taking stakeholder preferences into account, they represent nothing new. If, instead, the stakeholder doctrine is something distinctive, it refers to demands that organisations be run for the benefit of all their stakeholders, and that they be accountable to all their stakeholders. In that form, the stakeholder doctrine is incompatible with business and all substantive objectives, and undermines accountability and property rights; it subverts the duty of agents to principals, and the wealth-creating capabilities of business strictly understood. The stakeholder doctrine should, therefore, be firmly resisted.

Rejoinder

Will Hutton

Those who have persevered so far with this book will wonder if its quarry has the temerity to utter another word—so aggressive and dismissive have the five authors been about stakeholding. Yet the IEA, as befits its liberal tradition, has offered the victim the right of reply. It is an offer which I readily accept, and my thanks to the editor, David Green, for making it.

I suspect that some of the writers have for the first time in their professional lives come to believe in market failure. If *The State We're In* can sell approaching a quarter of million copies and one of its central propositions—stakeholding—can be championed, however cautiously, by a major political party, then something must be wrong with the marketplace for economic ideas and votes. Or alternatively the book-buying and voting public have been duped, and the mistakes and falsehoods must be exposed as quickly as possible. Hence this book.

There are some areas where we can profitably argue and some good points have been made by my critics—but in the main I have been cast as a deluded leftist/statist with the usual baggage of opinions that comes with such views, by writers who, while protesting their liberality of view and open-mindedness, are themselves steeped in ideology. I suspect that Sir Stanley Kalms, Conservative party-fundraiser, quangoholder extraordinary and quintessential member of the Conservative nomenklatura, will not see the joke that a man as enmeshed as himself in political partisanship and rule by executive fiat is speaking from experience when he claims to see a disquieting similarity between my ideas and those of pre-Yeltsin Russia; this is truly a case of the pot calling the kettle black, although I do not admit to even being the kettle of Kalm's imagination. I confess I laughed out loud when I read his contribution. Small wonder the Conservative party do not understand the nature of the political avalanche that has hit them; to imagine that being critical of the Conservatives places the critic in the same political universe as Soviet communism is weird. The new debate is how to shape the institutions, incentives and legal framework of a capitalist economy. There is as much capitalism in my thinking as any socialism—indeed the attempt to break out of the old antagonisms is bound to mean some incorporation of both—and there are plenty to the left of me who believe that the body of ideas around stakeholding is dangerous precisely because it will make the capitalist economy work better and with less social pain—and so save capitalism from itself.

Sir Stanley and I do not see eye to eye on that; nor on much else. As for his unalloyed hymn of praise to British retailers, if you are as tall as me you might take a more sceptical view. Sir Stanley should join me on a shopping expedition looking for trousers, jackets and shirts in Hamburg compared with a comparable British town, say, Bristol. The choice and quality in German shops is outstanding across the size range; in Britain the quest for high volume to meet the rent and dividend demands of the institutional savers who own the bulk of our high street property and the shares of our retailers means that the large, or small, male is poorly served by contrast with his counterparts in Germany. What is on offer is the commodity product tailored for standard sizes, that yields high volume turnover, at which British retailers are good. It is the same story with electrical goods. If you want a commodity electrical good—a bog standard radio or camera—you might shop at Dixons; but if you have more customised demands, the chain is not for you—and has probably competed out of business the local photographic or electrical shop who might have served your interest. There are losses to be offset against the gains of current British retailing. Sorry Sir Stanley, I can imagine you fuming at these 'stakeholder' thoughts—but I'm not the only one to have them.

The skirmishes with the Chairman of Dixons are not just an amusing trading of blows; in some respects they go to the heart of the matter. David Green may be more subtle in his essay than Sir Stanley, but his basic point remains the same. I am 'a system-design socialist', Green alleges, who wants governments to do what individuals should do for themselves, and so betrays the classic-liberal ideal—the reinvigoration of civil society. I may have escaped the worst heresies of twentieth century labourism and socialism, but I am still a meddler whose insistence on social inclusion means that I want to second-guess markets and the results of individual choices. Worse, by using compulsory state power I chase out voluntary organisations and the results of voluntary co-operation.

Green accuses me of being an ideological man of the left; let me return the accusation. I do not believe in utopias and top-down blueprints; its one of the reasons I do not describe myself as a socialist and why I have been so critical of the utopians of the New Right. Yet although David Green makes a useful point in arguing that there were more strands in Conservatism over the last eighteen years than I allow, and many of the 'free-market' notions were improperly followed, there is a clear organising principle that spans initiatives as disparate as establishing the internal market in the NHS or deregulating the financial system. These were 'Tory system-designers' who believed in the top-down implementation of individualistic contract as the best model to organise both the health service and the financial system. The system designers may have made compromises along the way, but there is no disputing their end or the economic thinking that underpinned it. I argue that this was driven by no less an ideological world view as that of any socialist.

I find it curious that I should be regarded as somehow not preoccupied with the invigoration of civil society; it is my over-riding concern—and propels my thinking whether it is my advocacy of constitutional reform or my desire to minimise inequality. Indeed it is stunning that in the five essays aimed at rebutting my work not one has addressed the central social fact of our times; growing inequality and its consequences. Here there is the starkest of differences between us. My view is that the growth of inequality is a far more potent explanation of the social forces that David Green and I both deplore and is deeply embedded in the quick of the market processes that all the writers so uncritically celebrate. There are such differences in power and knowledge between contracting parties in markets, and such insuperable difficulties in designing contracts so they take into account the impact on third parties now and in the future, that we know *a priori* that markets will get themselves into a fix—and that inequality of income is one of the inevitable by-products. The unskilled get trapped at the bottom, moving from unemployment to semi-employment and back again—while winner-take-all effects drive incomes skyward at the top. If we cherish non-market values, as David Green agrees, then these processes sustain an ugly new value system at both ends of the income scale; from active hostility to civil society at the bottom to disdainful opting out at the top. If a civil community is constructed on powers of empathy and bonds of reciprocity, growing inequality is one sure way of undermining it.

It's not sufficient to fall back on the Hayekian let-out that markets are processes of uncertain experimentation and should not be seen as tending to points of perfect balance; so they are—but that doesn't mean that society cannot have a view on whether the experimentation is working well or not, and be able to express a view about alternative outcomes through voting. Such judgements, because they are expressed through state institutions, should not be seen as enemies of civil society and true liberalism; rather they are the essential way democracy and capitalism operate hand in hand.

One of the alarming aspects of some of the diatribes vented against stakeholding in this book is their essentially anti-democratic nature; the only use of public power, in their lexicon, is to guarantee that private options are maximised and unhindered. Any other use of public action, even if initiated by democratically won power, is allegedly illiberal. This is free-market totalitarianism.

In any case it is absurd to argue that the ills of our times—from family breakdown to the emergence of a large underclass—are solely the result of the malign use of public power. The trends in the British labour market, producing the 30/30/40 society (see pp. 6-7) are intimately bound up with income distribution, life chances and social experience. The growth of hard drug-taking on the our large social housing estates is not solely because the state provides the incentive; it is at least in part because upward mobility from the bottom twenty per cent of British society is nigh impossible—and the teenagers and young adults in these positions know it. Drug-taking, at first a diversion of a few, becomes acceptable by the many; and the problem grows explosively.

Equally if de-industrialisation has removed the workplaces where young men were socialised and sanctioned for anti-social behaviour, then it is perverse to blame the social security system for not providing an alternative. In my recent book, *The State To Come*, I show how the sacking of bus-conductors—rational in terms of economic logic for deregulated private bus operators —has unpleasant side-effects from traffic congestion to the decreasing safety of buses. In a pure market contracting model these cannot be accounted for; to argue that a political process which acts as a countervailing power is an attack on voluntary organisations or moral behaviour is just odd. Or is this an argument against the political process altogether, at any time or place?

It is across this divide that the five writers' pieces have to be seen, even that of economist Tim Congdon whose article seems the most based in facts and theory. His is the most perplexing and offbeam contribution of all. My argument is that British companies set very demanding financial criteria for new investment; they are underborrowed by international comparison; and that this has an important role in influencing the character and level of new investment. I also predict that although the rate of investment is poor, the intense financial pressures originating in the financial system cause companies to make their existing assets work hard. I therefore predict that Britain's financial system will deliver high productivity of the existing stock of capital but that the stock itself will be small and grow very only slowly; moreover because investment and therefore growth is poor, and with low levels of borrowing, by contrast I would expect the financial returns on capital to be poor.

Indeed when I was working on *The State to Come*, the follow-up book to *The State We're In*, I drafted a section showing that my view on short-termism was the only plausible way to explain these apparently inconsistent figures. It was with a wry smile that I read Tim's piece, in which he contrived to make the same figures prove the exact opposite! His capacity to get things back to front is underlined by his triumphant claim that Peter Young—the investment manager at Morgan Grenfell disgraced for manipulating his unit trust values—was acting precisely in the stakeholder, committed fashion I advocate because so much of the fund was investment in unquoted, illiquid securities. He finds it funny, he says. But my argument is precisely the opposite. Mr Young, under intense pressure to deliver high financial performance over a short period of time, was locked into a competitive vortex—cemented by a salary and bonus structure—in which to make such returns he was forced to manipulate share values in offshore regulatory havens. I offer a theory in which Mr Young's conduct makes perfect sense in terms of the incentives in the system and which also explains high productivity of capital, low investment and poor financial returns. This may be why the book sells in such numbers; a lot of people think that the description I offer of the interaction of Britain's structure of corporate ownership, company law, tax system and highly liquid stock market on corporate behaviour very persuasive—a lot more plausible than Tim's view that the British financial system is the acme of perfection and all defects originate in clumsy state-driven intervention.

Which is why I come to advocate stakeholder capitalism. I agree with both Green and Ricketts who say that the aim should be to have a variety of ownership models spanning mutuality, the public limited company and even state owned companies—but I wonder where they have been living the last few years. Mutuality is rapidly disappearing, and privatisation of state companies is culling another ownership structure; the joint stock company, 70 per cent of whose equity is owned by pension funds and insurance companies, is the overwhelming form of organisation of private firms in Britain. My argument is that this financial and ownership architecture helps breed a short-termist, deal-driven capitalism in which excessive risk is displaced onto workforces—who have little protection in law. Thus there are growing numbers of insecure jobs as work becomes bundled up into commoditised units to be bought and sold—a denial of the humanity of work, and very obstructive in building the relationships of trust that permit far sighted investment.

Elaine Sternberg dislikes the whole idea because stakeholding qualifies property rights and dilutes the proper managerial aim of profit maximisation. She is right. Stakeholding is founded on the principle, deeply rooted in Christian Europe, that property is a privilege whose rights have accompanying obligations. No good society can permit those who own great concentrations of private property to exercise their rights without any countervailing recognition that their actions may have unfortunate or undesired consequences on others. The best order is one which regulates itself voluntarily, so that private property holders exercise their privileges judiciously and fairly; but a prudent society has the backstop of a legal framework to offer the capacity to intervene as a last resort. Martin Ricketts, whose survey of current economic literature I found rather selective, will be familiar with the growing body of literature on game theory and contracting that supports such a contention.

In any case Sternberg's view that the current structure of British company law offers directors an uncomplicated duty to maximise profit is innocence born of little experience of corporate boardrooms. Most directors are painfully aware of how they have to juggle the competing claims of the various stakeholders. Finding the right balance between allocating any given productivity gain to lower prices, higher wages or greater dividends is highly delicate. The trouble in the British context is that the shareholder interest overwhelms other stakeholders' interests, frequently to the long-run detriment of the company; very few directors regard the notion that a whole company should revolve around the notion of maximising the earnings per share as any other but tyrannous. There are a host of ways of measuring corporate performance, but they are being steadily downgraded.

Stakeholding makes these choices that underlie the governance of corporations more explicit, while aiming to provide an ownership structure in which there can be more genuine choice about the culture and character of firms than at present. I boggle at the suggestion that this is socialist system-design. The obligations that accompany the privilege of trading with limited liability have been set down in various Companies Acts; stakeholding involves a recasting of this framework in which private enterprise takes place. We change the rules of football or cricket to improve the quality of the game; we can change the rules by which capitalism is played too. If we can't, what kind of democracy is it? This perhaps is the most dangerous of the underlying presumptions that underpin all the five writers' views. They proclaim choice, but they only believe in one choice; they protest pluralism, but only if it leads to one outcome. They scoff at the notion that British capitalism can be improved, believing that its underperformance is wholly because of malign byproducts of state intervention. Popper warned that the enemies of the

Open Society were those who adopted non-falsifiable thought constructs—and while the IEA can be excused of that charge in generously encouraging a free exchange of views under its own aegis, some of my critics in this volume seem to me to come dangerously close to holding non-falsifiable positions. They are beginning to resemble the very enemies of the Open Society to whom they themselves believe they are opposed. The wheel is turning full circle.

Notes

How Britain Benefits from Short-termism

1 Hutton, W. *The State We're In*, London: Jonathan Cape, 1995, p. 21.

2 *Ibid*, p. 66.

3 *Ibid*, p. 25.

4 Macfarlane, A., *The Culture of Capitalism*, Oxford: Basil Blackwell, 1987, especially chapter 8, pp. 170-90, on 'The cradle of capitalism—the case of England'.

5 Hutton, *op. cit.*, pp. 132-33.

6 *Ibid.*, p. 134.

7 Tobin, J., 'A proposal for international monetary reform', *Eastern Economic Journal*, vol. 4, no. 3, 1978.

8 Moggridge, D. and Johnson, E. (eds.), *The Collected Writings of John Maynard Keynes*, vol. VII, *The General Theory* (originally published in 1936), Basingstoke: Macmillan, 1973, pp. 155, 160. So Keynes anticipated Hutton's phrase 'the fetish of liquidity'. Hutton refers to Keynes not in chapter six, but in chapter nine, 'Why Keynesian economics is best', especially pp. 239-45. Hutton's previous book, *The Revolution That Never Was*, London: Longman, 1986, is all about Keynes.

9 Hutton, *op. cit.*, p. 157.

10 *Ibid*, p. 157.

11 *Ibid*, p. 158.

12 Miles, D., 'Testing for short termism in the UK stock market', *Economic Journal*, vol. 103, no. 4, 1993, cited in Hutton, *op. cit.*, p. 160.

13 Hutton, *op. cit.*, pp. 166-67.

14 Markowitz, H.M., 'Portfolio selection', *Journal of Finance*, vol. 7, no. 1, 1952, pp. 77-91.

15 Arrow has identified a social benefit from financial markets, using the mean-variance model. Where liquid financial markets help investors to diversify their portfolios, they improve the private and social trade-offs between risk and return. See Arrow, K.J., *Collected Papers of K.J. Arrow: The*

Economics of Information, Oxford: Basil Blackwell, 1984, p. 79. The idea originally appeared in the 1965 Yrjo Jahnsson lectures.

16 Congdon, T.G., 'The role of central banking in economic development', *The Review of Policy Issues*, vol. 2, no. 2, 1996, pp. 82-86.

17 John R. Hicks suggested a distinction between 'fluid' and 'solid' investors, developing ideas originally expressed in 1974 lectures on *The Crisis in Keynesian Economics*. Fluid investors like the flexibility conferred by holding liquid assets in their portfolios, whereas solid investors are less keen on it. In principle, degrees of liquidity-aversion could be measured, just as with risk-aversion. (Hicks, J.R., *The Market Theory of Money*, Oxford: Clarendon Press, 1989.)

18 Goldsmith, R.W., *Financial Structure and Development*, New Haven and London: Yale University Press, 1969. See, for example, p. 40 which contains the remark, the 'existence of clearly different paths of financial development is doubtful. The evidence now available is more in favour of the hypothesis that thee exists only one major path of financial development, a path marked by certain regularities in the course of the financial interrelations ratio, in the share of financial institutions in total financial assets and in the position of the banking system.' (The financial interrelations ratio is the ratio of financial assets to tangible assets.) Goldsmith's point is that the historical record demonstrates that the FIR and the relative importance of financial institutions in the economy increase with incomes per head.

19 Note that Hutton implicitly assumes diminishing marginal returns on capital and imperfect international mobility of capital. Both assumptions are plausible, but—in a world of increasing international capital mobility—the pressure (if any) from British investors on British companies for high returns would be less effective, since the companies of any nation could tap global capital markets. A radical criticism of Hutton's thesis is that, as the abolition of exchange controls leads increasingly to global capital market integration, the portfolio preferences of specifically British investors will become irrelevant to the financial targets of British companies.

20 For details of this work, contact the author at Lombard Street Research.

Will Hutton and Welfare Reform

1 Hutton, W., *The State We're In*, London: Jonathan Cape, 1995, p. 195.

2 *Ibid.*, p. 310.

3 *Ibid.*, p. 309.

4 *Ibid.*, p. 311.

5 *Ibid.*, p. 306.

6 *Ibid.*, p. 310.

7 *Ibid.*, p. 311.

8 *Ibid.*, p. 169.

9 *Ibid.*, p. 225.

10 *Ibid.*, p. 175.

11 *Ibid.*, p. 226.

12 *Ibid.*, p. 226.

13 *Social Trends 27*, London: HMSO, 1997, Table 8.4

14 Hutton, p. 230.

15 *Ibid.*, p. 175.

16 *Ibid.*, p. 174.

17 *Ibid.*, p. 60.

18 Smith, *Wealth of Nations*, p. 610.

19 Phillips, M., *All Must Have Prizes*, London: Little Brown, 1996.

20 Röpke, W., *A Humane Economy*, London: Oswald Wolff, 1960, p. 125.

21 Hutton, p. 311.

22 *Ibid.*, p. 310.

23 *Ibid.*, p. 173.

24 Bosanquet, H., *The Strength of the* People, London: Macmillan, 1903, 2nd edition, p. 110.

25 *Ibid.*, p. 110.

26 *Ibid.*, p. 94.

27 *Ibid.*, p. 92.

28 *Ibid.*, p. 18.

29 *Ibid.*, pp. 175-76.

30 *Ibid.*, p. 326.

31 *Ibid.*, p. 172.

32 *Ibid.*, p. 126.

33 Hill, O., extract from 'Letter to My Fellow-Workers: Work Among the Poor During 1884 & 1885'.

34 See Hayek, F.A., *Law, Legislation and Liberty*, London: Routledge, 1979, vol. 3, p. 50.

35 Prochaska, F.K., *Philanthropy and the Hospitals of London*, Oxford: Clarendon Press, 1992; Green, D., *Working-Class Patients and the Medical Establishment*, Aldershot: Gower, 1985.

36 Green, D.G., 'From National Health Monopoly to National Health Guarantee', in Gladstone, D. (ed.), *Personal Payment for Healthcare: Empowering the Patient or Blaming the Victim?*, London: IEA Health and Welfare Unit, forthcoming.

37 Le Grand, J., 'Liberty, Equality and Vouchers' in *Empowering the Parents: How to Break the Schools Monopoly*, London: IEA Health and Welfare Unit, 1991.

38 Hutton, p. 310.

Market Theory, Competition and the Stakeholder Society

1 Hutton, W., *The State We're In*, London: Jonathan Cape, 1995, p.237.

2 *Ibid.*, p. 111.

3 *Ibid.*, p. 239.

4 *Ibid.*, p. 244.

5 Schumpeter, J.A., *Capitalism, Socialism and Democracy*, London: Unwin University Books, 1943.

6 Hayek, F.A., 'The Use of Knowledge in Society', *American Economic Review*, Vol. 35, 1945, pp. 519-30.

7 Shackle, G.L.S., *Expectation, Enterprise and Profit: The Theory of the Firm*, London: Allen and Unwin, 1970.

8 Wiseman, J., 'Uncertainty, Costs and Collectivist Economic Planning', *Economica*, May, 1953.

9 Loasby, B.J., *Choice, Complexity and Ignorance*, Cambridge University Press, 1976.

10 Kirzner, I., *Competition and Entrepreneurship*, University of Chicago Press, 1973.

11 Coase, R., 'The Nature of the Firm', *Economica*, Vol.4, No.16, 1937, pp. 386-405.

12 Alchian, A., *Economic Forces at Work*, Liberty Press Indianapolis, 1977.

13 Demsetz, H., *Ownership, Control and the Firm: The Organisation of Economic Activity*, Basil Blackwell, 1988.

14 Williamson, O.E., *The Economic Institutions of Capitalism: Firms, Markets, Relational Contracting*, London: Collier Macmillan, 1985.

15 Hutton, *op. cit.*, p. 249.

16 *Ibid.*, p. 256.

17 *Ibid.*, p. 277.

18 *Ibid.*, p. 285.

19 *Ibid.*, p. 250.

20 *Ibid.*, p. 252.

21 Hirschman, A., *Exit, Voice and Loyalty: Responses to Decline in Firms Organizations and States*, Harvard University Press, 1970.

22 Hechter, M., *Principles of Group Solidarity*, Berkeley, Los Angeles: University of California Press, 1987.

23 For an extended discussion of the evolution of conventions, see Sugden, R., *The Economics of Rights, Cooperation and Welfare*, Oxford: Basil Blackwell, 1986.

24 Mochizuki, K., 'Tomorrow's Capitalism in a Japanese Perspective', *RSA Journal*, October, 1994, pp. 37-45.

25 *Ibid.*, p. 39.

26 Mikuni, A., 'The Nikkei: A Casualty of Japan's Outmoded Economy', *Wall Street Journal Europe*, August 1992, p. 6.

27 Ubukata, Y., 'Stepping Out of the Pyramid', *Intersect*, Vol. 7, No. 3, pp. 18-24.

28 *Ibid.*, p. 22.

29 'Japan encourages its young', Management Focus, *The Economist*, 10 August 1991, p. 57.

30 Mochizuki, *op. cit.*

31 Clark, R.L. and Ogawa, N., 'Employment Tenure and Earnings Profiles in Japan and the United States: Comment', *American Economic Review*, Vol. 82, No. 1, 1992, pp. 336-45.

32 Wagstyl, S., 'The Big Squeeze in Japan', *Financial Times*, Monday 27 April 27 1992.

33 Office of the Chief Economist of the United States' Securities and Exchange Commission, 1985. Also McConnell, J.J. and Muscarella, C.J., 'Corporate Capital Expenditure Decisions and the Market Value of the Firm', *Journal of Financial Economics*, Vol. 14, 1985, pp. 399-422.

34 Hall, B.H., 'Effects of Takeover Activity on Corporate Research and Development', in Auerbach, A.J. (ed.), *Corporate Takeovers: Causes and Consequences*, Chicago: NBER, University of Chicago Press, 1988, pp. 69-96.

35 Bid premia averaged about 30 per cent in the mid 1980s.

36 Jensen, M.C., 'Takeovers: Their Causes and Consequences', *Journal of Economic Perspectives*, Vol. 2, No. 1, 1988, pp. 21-48.

37 This theory has become known as the 'free cash flow' theory of takeovers.

38 Schranz, M.S., 'Takeovers Improve Firm Performance: Evidence from the Banking Industry', *Journal of Political Economy*, Vol. 101, No. 2, pp. 299-326.

39 Jenkins, S., *Accountable to None - The Tory Nationalisation of Britain*, London: Hamish Hamilton, 1995.

40 North, D.C., *Institutions, Institutional Change and Economic Performance*, Cambridge University Press, 1990.

41 Robertson, D. and Dennison, S., *The Control of Industry*, Cambridge Economic Handbook, Nisbet, Cambridge University Press, 1960.

42 See, for example, 'In general, whoever has a value that has become firm-specific will seek some form of control over the firm', in Alchian, A. and Woodward, S., 'Reflections on the Theory of the Firm' *Journal of Institutional and Theoretical Economics*, Vol. 143, No. 1, 1987, pp. 119-20.

Stakeholder Theory: The Defective State It's In

1 Unless otherwise specified, all page references are to the Hutton essay as it appears in this volume.

2 For an analysis of why, for example, Hutton's approach to 'short-termism' is wrong, see Sternberg, E., *Just Business: Business Ethics in Action*, Little, Brown, 1994; Warner paperback, 1995, especially pp. 204-6 and 177; and Davies, S., 'Short-termism and The State We're In', Institute of Directors, 1996.

3 In an internal memo at the Stanford Research Institute (now SRI International, Inc.); see Freeman, R.E., *Strategic Planning: a Stakeholder Approach*, Pitman Publishing, 1984, p. 31.

4 *Ibid*, p. 46.

5 *Ibid*, p. 52.

6 E.g., the rainforests.

7 Those allegedly threatened by the disposal of Brent Spar at the bottom of the ocean.

8 The future generations, of whatever species, in whose name ecologists protest against various perceived depredations.

9 Most of the criticisms that will be presented would, however, apply even if 'stakeholders' referred only to shareowners, employees, suppliers, lenders, and customers.

10 For a full analysis of this conception of business, see Sternberg, E., *Just Business*, *op. cit.*, especially Chapter 2.

11 Or to justify some other principle of allocation.

12 Typically that set out in the corporation's Memorandum of Association or comparable constitutional document; one way to improve corporate governance is to frame the corporate

purpose more narrowly than has traditionally been the case.

13 More generally, organisational governance refers to methods of keeping organisations to the purposes established by their owners/funders.

14 For an analysis of why the German and Japanese models of corporate governance are inferior to the Anglo-Saxon model, see Sternberg, E., *Corporate Governance: Accountability in the Marketplace*, IEA, forthcoming.

15 Though it (and more generally an organisation) may render itself accountable to other parties through contractual arrangements. The fact that, e.g., businesses can be held to account by government is a function of the coercive power of government, not its notional role as stakeholder. The extent to which government has any *right* to control business in this way is a key issue of political philosophy.

16 Kay, J., 'The root of the matter', *Financial Times*, 16 February 1996, p. 17.

17 Which even when properly understood cannot sustain a viable ethical theory; see, e.g., MacIntyre, A., *After Virtue: a study in ethical theory*, Gerald Duckworth & Co. Ltd, 1981.

18 This section draws heavily on Sternberg, E., *Just Business, op. cit.*, pp. 39-40, 50.

19 Although individuals typically retain the right to self-defence.

20 By conscription into the armed forces, and in some jurisdictions through capital punishment.

21 Subject, of course, to fulfilling any contractual commitments they might have undertaken.

22 See Sternberg, E., *Just Business, op. cit.*, especially pp. 41-42.

23 That corporations are indeed the property of their shareholders is discussed more fully in Sternberg, E., *Corporate Governance: Accountability in the Marketplace, op. cit.*

24 For a full explanation and justification of these concepts, see *ibid*, especially Chapter 3. Briefly, distributive justice exists when organisational rewards reflect contributions made to the organisational objective. Ordinary decency is not

generalised 'niceness', but the conditions of trust necessary for operating over the long term: honesty, fairness, the avoidance of physical violence and coercion, and a presumption of legality.

25 *Ibid*, pp. 256-57.

26 For a full discussion of social responsibility see *ibid*, Chapter 10, pp. 254-61.